Nottinghamshire Miners' Tales

Angela Franks

A celebration of life in the Nottinghamshire coalfields during the twentieth century

**Published by
Reflections of a Bygone Age
Keyworth, Nottingham
2001**
Printed by Adlard Print & Reprographics Ltd
Ruddington, Nottingham

ISBN 1 900138 63 8

Dedication
I wish to dedicate this book to all the miners of Nottinghamshire and to my husband, Greg, for his practical help, support and encouragement. He soon discovered that there is no such thing as a free lunch.

Old money and measurements
Before currency was decimalised in 1971 money was divided into
£ (pounds) s (shillings) and d (pence).
There were:
20s to the pound and 12d to the shilling.
A shilling was often referred to as a 'bob'
Sixpence was called a 'tanner'
2/6d was known as 'half a crown'.
£1/1s was a guinea.
In decimal currency 1p is the equivalent of 2.4d
5p = 1shilling and 50p = 10s.

When Sid Radford bought a packet of Woodbines for 2d in 1930 the modern equivalent would be less than 1p. Today in 2001 a cheap packet of cigarettes costs £3.85p.

The old measurements were expressed as:
12 inches = 1foot
3 feet   = 1yard (36inches)
A metre is slightly longer than a yard so the 9 yard stint which Neal Kirk describes in 1944 would be approximately 8.75 metres

Acknowledgements:
My most grateful thanks to all those who agreed to be interviewed - without them the book would not exist; my sister, Irene Short, for applying her considerable skills to the typing of the transcripts; the Local Studies Library, Nottinghamshire, for permission to use transcripts from their collection; Groggs, for allowing me to use pictures of the collier figures; McChrystal Snuff for the use of their advertising material; the National Museum of Labour History, the *Hucknall Dispatch, Nottingham Evening Post,* U.K. Coal and the DTI for help with the photographs; Stan Stanton, Mick Noble, and Norman Beadle for the loan and use of photographs and ephemera, and my publishers, Reflections of a Bygone Age (Brian and Mary Lund).

Contents

Introduction — Page 4

Part One: — Page 5
THE EARLY DAYS – A Family Affair. The Job Interview. Getting There. Working on the Pit Top. Going Underground for the First Time. Gangers and Ponies. Snap and Break Time. Going Down the Roads. The Old Colliers.

Part Two: — Page 15
LIFE AT THE TOP – Keeping Clean. Spanish 'flu. The 1920s and the Strikes. The Dukeries. Pastimes. The Miners' Welfare. St. John's Ambulance. At the Area Finals.

Part Three: — Page 25
DEALING WITH EMERGENCIES – Accidents. Sid's Story. Two Remarkable Women. The Mines Rescue Service. Joining the Brigade. Summoned by Bells. Emergency at Doe Lea. Canaries. The Markham Disaster. Explosion at Thurcroft. Bringing Out the Injured.

Part Four: — Page 38
THE WAR YEARS AND AFTER – The Thirties. The Home Guard. Dunkirk. Careless Talk. Air Raids. Shortages. Bevin Boys. Nationalisation at Last.

Part Five: — Page 46
MECHANISATION – Problems and Complaints. The Old and the New. The Price of Progress. Industrial Illnesses. The *Evening Post* Campaign on behalf of the Miners. Nurses at the Pit.

Part Six: — Page 51
THE FIFTIES AND SIXTIES – Galas. Subsidence. The Honeymoon is Over. Competition from Oil and Gas. Sharing the Good Times and the Bad. Pithead Baths. Snuff. The Hoax Calls. Underwater Training. The Medical. Sports Day. The Welfare.

Part Seven: — Page 59
THE TURBULENT YEARS – The Job Interview 1970s Style. Working on the Pit Top at Hucknall. Underground at Cotgrave. 1970s Strike and Go Slow. An Incident at Stavely.

Part Eight: — Page 67
THE 1984-85 STRIKE – The Struggle Begins. The Contenders Comment. Violence Erupts. The Striking Miners. The Police. The Nottinghamshire Women's Support Group. The Right to a Ballot. The Pickets. The UDM. The Closures. Eastwood – the End of an Era. Trouble in the Council Chamber.

Part Nine: — Page 81
THE FINAL DECADE – The Robin Hood Line. The Challenge. The Coalfield Enquiry. Some Important Conclusions. Bilsthorpe. Moving On. Reclamation and Memorials. The Future of Coalmining in Nottinghamshire.

Introduction

'Nottinghamshire Miner's Tales' recounts the experiences of the men who worked in the county's coalfields. It is a story of endurance and courage in a hostile environment, set against a backdrop of the great events and upheavals of the twentieth century. As the heavy industries disappeared or diminished, the miners became the last men to undertake such exhausting physical work in dangerous conditions. They were often undervalued and sometimes badly led, but it was their daily struggle that created the bonds of humour, friendship and compassion for which the mining communities became famous.

Most of the county's pits have vanished, and monuments are gradually appearing across the county. But their significance will soon be lost, because memories are so short-lived that all can be forgotten within the space of one generation. However, through words and pictures, the story can be saved for posterity.

In 'Nottinghamshire Miners' Tales' the anecdotes of colliers themselves provide both a narrative and a tribute. But, be warned, miners usually have a twinkle in their eye. *'Miners' tales me duck. To be taken with a pinch of snuff.'*

Angela Franks
November 2001

Retired history teacher Angela Franks moved to Bingham, Nottinghamshire, with her husband and three sons. She soon felt at home in her adopted county as she discovered its long association with coal mining. For Angela was born and raised in South Wales, where her grandfather and uncle worked in the heavy industries which developed alonside the coal mines. As a very young child, she firmly believed that all hills were actually spoil tips!

"Meeting the miners and their families has been a privilege," says Angela, "and I hope to tell more stories of the men and women of Nottinghamshire in future versions of Nottinghamshire Tales."

Angela's other interests include music and theatre, which Nottingham provides in abundance.

PART ONE: The Early Days

A Family Affair
'Does your father work 'ere?'

Speaking in March 2001, Geoff Blore, who left Newstead Colliery in 1987, said:
"Both my sons were in mining but now the eldest one is a software engineer for British Aerospace and the younger one runs the Night Shelter on Canal Street."

Norman Beadle, who was in the Mines Rescue Service until 1994 said:
"My younger son is a whizz with all this computer stuff and the older one is at Nottingham University studying English. He wants to be a teacher."

But in the early days, mining was very much a family affair, which had a great impact on family life as Mr Instone, who was born in 1902, recalls:
" ...... my father was a butty. That entailed employing men to get the coal....... On Friday my mother used to go to Eastwood Hall to collect the wages and then she'd bring them home and the men would all congregate around the table at home and he would pay them out and sometimes he had to go upstairs to fetch some of his own money to pay them out."

It was also passed down through many generations. The sons of miners became miners and their daughters married miners.

Harold Henshaw, born in 1894 and interviewed at Arnold in 1984, recalls:
"My father was a colliery manager. He and all his brothers were colliery officials. In other words we've been in mining as far back as I can trace."

Sid Radford, born in 1916 ;
".... the family came here into Nottingham from Derbyshire for a shilling a day more. .....three brothers and a father all down Sherwood. We were all at Sherwood."

For mining in Nottinghamshire was always comparatively well paid.

The Job Interview

The job interview also followed a pattern.
Fred Simpson, referring here to 1922 when he was thirteen years of age and went for a job at Mansfield:
"Well me father said go to the colliery at a certain time and in the morning I went up there and there was a few boys stood about and someone came to me, somebody named Spencer. He says, 'Have you come for a job lad?' I says yes. He says, 'Well follow me.' He took me in to see the manager and the under-manager

Geoff Blore

Nottinghamshire Miners' Tales

who was setting on, a Mr Davis, Fred Davis, and he said did me father work there and I said yes and I told him who I was and I got the job and I started work on the Wednesday."

Sid's version is a little more complicated. He was the youngest, and his parents were reluctant to let him go into mining, so he spent seven weeks between Easter and Whitsun, in 1930:

".... looking all round Mansfield, factories, foundries, metal box, wagon works........I went out looking for a job every day, couldn't get one."

Eventually he and his Dad went to the pit. "*Went to see Mr. Heathcote on a Saturday morning. Mr Heathcote was the manager and he had got one eye. Knocked on his office door, cap off, ready to go in. 'Come in.' Off I went in and with one eye he had to look round like that you see and he said to my Dad, 'Hello Matty. Whatever can I do for you?' And my Dad said to him, 'Well Mr Heathcote, I've come to see if this lad can have a job in the shops.' Now shops at the pit top was where they mended tubs that the coal came in and they sharpened picks. It was like blacksmiths work with a forge and all that. He came round and he said to my Dad.*

Now Matty, you know these jobs are only for deputy's sons.' Because a deputy was classed nearly as a god in those days. Well that's what he said and we had to come out of the office. No job."

But seven weeks later and still without a job, Sid returned to the pit. His father told him where to go and who to see:

"*He said, 'Well you go up some steps that are called the gantry and on top of these steps you'll see there's an office and that's where you go for a job. And it'll be Mr. Martin, he's the boss and you'll know him because he'll have a bowler hat on.' Anyway I get just to the top of the steps, about thirty steps, quite high, and this bloke's coming out of the office with a bowler hat on so I got up to him and I said is it Mr. Martin?*

He said,' Yes. What do you want?' I said I wondered if you had a vacancy on the screens. He said, 'Does your father work 'ere?' I said yes he does. He said, 'What's his name?' I said Matty Radford. He said,' Oh yes. I know Matty. Come back this afternoon.' I had just walked three miles there so I had to walk three miles back. I said to him shall I bring my snap tin? He looked at me and he said,' 'Well if you feel like that you'd bloody better.' That's how I got my job at Sherwood."

Getting There

So how did everyone get to work?
Sid: "*We walked to work. Nobody ever rode;*

Sid Radford, photographed in the 1940s

6   Nottinghamshire Miners' Tales

very few had got a bike. There was only one car at Sherwood when I started and that was the Manager's."

Bill, talking about 1938 when he started: "*I worked at Rufford Colliery which was about five miles from Mansfield. ..... walked there through the forest and came right out in the pit colliery yard. But when I had regular wages of about 30 shillings I was able to travel on the bus at 6d a day return.*"

Working on the Pit Top.
'Goes by at a hell of a racket.'
Sid describes working on the screens:
"*You sorted the coal as it went by on a big (metal) belt, four feet wide. Goes by at a hell of a racket, can't hear yourself. When you first started you used to work with sign language. You used to stop there sorting this bat out. You used to put it in a bin at the back of you. In fact you used to go as fast as this (signing). Sorting bat out all day, fourteen hours .....Bat is the waste. Some call it bat, some call it muck. It was like slate. .... I started on Monday and I got one shift two shillings and fivepence in old money. The next week I got six shifts in – twelve shillings and sixpence. I was the biggest bloody man that this town's ever known.*"

Sid handed all his earnings over to his Mum just as he always had since he was eleven and had started his paper round. To his amazement, his mother now doubled his pocket money to one shilling a week.

The screens at East Kirkby (Summit) Colliery on a c. 1906 picture postcard. The picture shows the primitive conditions in the screening sheds, which hardly changed for decades. Once on the surface, coal was transferred to the screens, rubble was removed, and the coal graded before being loaded onto the waiting wagons. It was back-breaking and low paid work, given to older or disabled miners and boys

Sid:
"Were I well off! Twopence for a packet of Woodbine and I had still got 10d left."

Mr Instone started work in the pit yard at Gedling in 1916 and had a very different job.

"I was in the time office in the first place and men used to check in. They used to have brass checks numbered and I'd got a board with all the numbers on and hooks and as they came along we used to have to hang the checks on the number and the timekeeper could mark down they were present..... and I used to have to carry all these checks across the yard and hang 'em up in the checkweigh on the pit top."

The system certainly worked, as Bill who in 1939 was training to be an electrician at Rufford soon found out. He worked nights from 9pm till 6am.

"It was more usually 7am by the time you finished but unfortunately it came to a sudden stop. Got too efficient at it you see and got done too early and where the electrician's shop was, was the stables for the horses. Nice friendly animals they were too. Well we came in one morning the electrician and I, about five instead of seven. Quickest we'd done and we used to nip in and kip down with the horses for ten minutes which was forbidden to sleep in the colliery. So at seven we were still asleep with the horses when the day shift came on. Couldn't find us 'cos one of the problems was you was checked in and checked out and if you hadn't come out there was a bit of a panic. Anyway got reprimanded for that and that led to me deciding to become one of the cutting team."

Going Underground for the First Time
'The man stood back and rang the signals and we dropped away like a stone.'

Without exception, miners young and old agreed the first trip to the pit bottom was terrifying. Sid's description is typical:

"I was frightened to death.... There is a bar you hold onto. Everybody just rests their arms on it. I'm sure I bent that bloody bar the first time I went down. I don't think I've ever been more frightened in my life.....
You would go down vroom like a bomb. Into dark out of light for a second or two and then into light again."

Fred Simpson was fourteen when he went down Mansfield pit for the first time in 1923.

"...It was like going to a football match because there was a tremendous lot of men and a tremendous lot of boys. I should think about

Grogg figure

1200 men used to work in a mine at that time of day….. There was a great mass of men waiting around a shaft there on the bank and I'm stood there with my Dad early in the morning. The pit bank was low girders because it had to allow for two gates for the cage, so you had to crouch. They all stood with their hands on the girders as though they were holding on. Actually they were crouching and taking the weight off their shoulders.

"You had to wait quite a while because the cage could only take 26 down at once. I'm stood there amongst this mass of men on this wood platform and I notice that these men appear to be holding on to these girders. I hadn't seen the cage. There was too many people around. I thought this platform here must be going down, rails the lot. I didn't know how deep the mine was so I put my hand on the girder and me father's at the side and he says,' What are you gripping that girder for?' He sensed I thought the lot was going down.

"When the crowd gradually moved away and I could see the gates open I realised that was the thing that went down. I got on the cage and we all huddled up and I realised for the first time I was going to have a real good drop and as soon as the gate was clanged to and the thing was chucked over the top to fasten it, the man stood back and rang the signals and we dropped away like a stone. And it was only when you got half way that a change came about. Your ears suddenly went as though you was deaf and you suddenly seemed to be coming back to the top. I noticed I could gradually see the lights from the pit bottom coming nearer and I realised we were still going down and then we got off and that's how my first day's work started."

Gangers and Ponies
'I didn't know one leather from the other. I was just mesmerised'
At first the lads spent a day clipping the empty tubs back onto the chain but soon they became gangers.
Sid:
"….in those days you didn't have training sessions. You were shown how to do a job and left. The same with the ponies. I had to ask for so and so, that was the corporal. I was sent pony driving and I hate bloody horses anyway. Then you have to walk about two miles to the coal face with this horse. A chap showed me how to gear this horse up. I didn't know one leather from the other. I was just mesmerised. 'And now you know how to do it don't you?' Of course I said yes but I didn't have the foggiest. It was two or three weeks before I learned to shackle him."

Most of them clearly remember the pony's name even decades later; 'Captain' seems to have been a favourite. The lads became very fond of their ponies and often gave them tit bits. In fact the only time Norman was ever caught scrumping was when he took an apple from the orchard for his pony. Another miner remembers regularly giving his pony a pinch of snuff which the animal came to prefer to the usual apple or carrot.

However, the job sounds straightforward enough. All a ganger had to do was amble back and forth between the coal face and the pit bottom; full tubs one way, empty tubs the other. But, like most things underground, there were many hazards. A small boy might be given a large horse. Putting a collar on him was difficult enough but if the ganger was working in low tunnels then he would have to dig out holes between the rails for the animal to walk in (dinting). Also the pony would become agitated because in a low tunnel it could injure its chine (backbone) on the beams. Then there were the doors which were there for ventilation. At one time boys, called trappers, were employed to let gangers through, but in the 1920s they had to sort it out for themselves.

Fred:

"The doors had got a half banded hoop so that when you pushed them open they bounced onto the first tub and as the second tub hit it they bounced again. Your pony was about to come through at a reasonable speed because it had got eight tubs at the back of him and of course there was a lot of weight there. Sometimes the horse would be right down on its haunches. So you had to hold the door and as the first tub was about to come you'd got to jump onto the limmer crank (behind the horse) now if you weren't quick enough you'd be nipped between the edge of the door and the first tub. As soon as your tub started bumping through you'd got to scramble off the limmers again, get by the horse as it was moving all the time, in sufficient time to open the next door and stand in position ready to drop onto the limmers for the second time."

This had to be done six times during each round trip and for at least eight runs a day, possibly ten or twelve if a boy was working for a big stall (area of coal face). Then there was cleaning the roadway and hauling supplies in the empty tubs. It is not surprising that accidents happened for gangers were also under pressure to go faster because of other lads and ponies coming behind. Sometimes tubs ran away and there was a series of smash ups. Fingers and hands, which were unprotected, were injured and occasionally horses were killed. Sid remembers a very sad case:

"There was a lad got killed on my job when I were on haulage. He got crushed by a couple of tubs which split him up into mincemeat. There were lumps of flesh all that day when I went on my job. Horrible. Frightening. All for about four bob a day. Terrible."

Ponies would also sweat profusely and develop sores which the lads often had to deal with. However the horses were well fed and well treated in the underground stables, and gradually protective gear was introduced for the animals. But everyone in the pit had to work very hard - ponies included. There was another bit of unpleasantness associated with the ponies.

Fred:

"They used to have corn boxes on the levels in the pit and water barrels sent and you used to fasten the horses there .... Food stuff used to come down in bags. And there were rats. Rats! And a lot used to come in the bags and you used to have to empty it into the mangers."

Ponies were protected by the Pit Ponies Protection Society and had an annual week's holiday when they were brought up from underground. At first their eyes were protected with blinkers until they became accustomed to the sunlight but they soon adjusted and enjoyed their week's freedom. The last ponies left the mines during the 1970s.

Archie the pit pony. After 26 years service, Archie retired to the Isle of Wight (photo: 'Coal' magazine October 1950)

"If the corporal was the right sort of fella' you'd get an extra run."

Sometimes an efficient ganger and corporal could earn extra money.
'You'd have a tip you see.'
Fred:
"If you were a good driver you always got back in time so you didn't keep the men waiting for empties. You'd have a tip you see. And if the corporal was the right sort of fella' and he was in with that particular stall you was driving to he'd always give you help to get running and by doing that you'd get an extra run during the turning of the day which probably meant another eight tubs or maybe two runs for the men in that stall so it meant they earned more money. …. They used to tip the ganger, they'd tip the corporal and other little tips for the deputy."

Then there was the business of keeping track of the tubs so each stall was paid for the coal it had produced.
Fred:
"….Every stall had its own individual number. If it was 52 stall they'd put 52 on. But If any went through unmarked they was always marked 13 at Mansfield Colliery because 13 was the colliery number. So the owners had a

lot of buckshee tubs. ….If tubs ran away down the plain, what you'd call a runaway, as they hit on one set they'd knock that off. You could get quite a series of smashed up tubs of coal and when they were refilled in a hurry some would be going without numbers and they of course went to number thirteen. So there was always a chance of men not being paid for what they did."

Snap and Break Time
'You had bread and dripping until you was bloody fed up of it.'
Sid:
"I took bread and dripping or bread and jam. Eight slices when you was a growing lad. You had bread and dripping until you were bloody fed up of it. And then you went onto jam and there was no snap tins then. You used newspaper. You used to take a drink in a bottle, a glass bottle, just plain water out of the tap. You used to fill it up before you went and put it in your pocket, a quart bottle. And later when you got to the coal face you had a dudley strapped on a rope on your back but the inside used to rust so you ended up drinking rust but of course you couldn't see it."
Fred:
"They only had a quarter of an hour break…… when it suited the corporal. If he'd got a few tubs in the passby and he wanted them out of the way he'd say, ' We'll take this break or we'll have you a snap bag.'"

It is not surprising that in the midst of all this hustle and bustle breakdowns and accidents were common.
Fred:
"….. only had a quarter of an hour break apart from if there was a serious breakdown in the pit somewhere or if the fan stopped ….. of course you could tell immediately the fan stopped before you had any message because everything was suddenly quiet because all the electrical apparatus has to be shut when there's no air 'cos if it's not fresh air it can have explosive mixtures in it. So everything used to go quiet and there was no noise of the wind rushing, whistling through the doors because you was always in movement of air. One side was cool and the other was too hot as it returned near the pit bottom. Now if the fan stopped you had to make your way to the main fresh air road. If it was going to be any length of time you used to have to withdraw because it (the fan) had got to run so long before you were allowed back in. That was the only chance you'd get of a little bit of a break. Or if someone had been killed maybe. Or a very nasty accident. Things would be stopped while they were getting the stretchers open. You might have a horse that would be crashed between one set of tubs and another simply because he came down a steepish way and the strap of his brecham (horse collar) might have broke and he couldn't hold his set of tubs. That horse would probably come over a previous set of tubs and perhaps be right down in a little tiny space and the little ganger lad a few yards ahead of him frightened to death because the horse was coming on top of him."

Going Down the Roads.
'You want to be a collier. We'll show you.'
Eventually the ganger was allowed to be part of the team at the coal face. The lads looked forward to doing a proper job at last but it was desperately important to do your stint like a man.

Bill, talking about the late 1930s:

"It was termed 'going down the roads' because the pit bottom was lit up and it meant going down into the dark, an exciting thought for a young fella' and so off I went. I was put on one of the faces and they said 'Right lad, you want to be a collier, we'll show you. You stop with him at that gate end and he'll show you how you go on, that chappie there. And your job's to clean them belts. Keep them clear while he's chopping his coal out an' that and you'll be alright.' Well I started to clear. This chap came and showed me. He says, 'You're alright lad, this is how you do it.' Ten shovels and it was clear. And I thought oh it's not so bad at all and I bent down to clear it and gradually it crept up me legs to me knees. 'What's the matter lad?' I can't cope wi' this I says. ' I'll show you. Give us your shovel.' So he came and appeared again. 'There y'are.'

Well ten minutes later and still up to me knees, I said I can't keep this up and he shouted something down to somebody else who shouted to somebody else, 'Put your sprags back in lads.' And I found that these other lads to the tune of about 150 yards away had all lifted the boards up on the belt so that all their slack and that was coming to me and since it was the end of the belt it was me had to move it. So I chucked the shovel down and I climbed off the face and I sat in there and cried and cried and cried. Backache, despondent and everything else. But the comfort of the chappie that was training me, he said,' C'mon lad you'll be alright.' And he was right. I mastered it. I'd learnt me lesson with the others. They didn't work it on me again like that."

The Old Colliers.
'He was 67 and still working with a pick and shovel.'
There are also vivid memories of the characters who 'broke them in.'

Sid:

"I was mad keen because we was thinking of getting married, I wanted that extra shilling a day so I asked to go on the coal face at nineteen. And I didn't go on the coal face I went to work with an old bloke who was making a drift. Now a drift is a tunnel going downhill. You make it. You don't follow a coal seam, you go downhill one in five from halfway up a shaft to the pit bottom. That was what they sent me to do with this old fellow who was 67 years old. There was no retirement in those days you know. He was 67 and still working with a pick and shovel. Old Arthur. You might only go three yards in a week. And we passed eleven seams of coal all from six inches to a foot until you got to the one they wanted to work which was one foot three inches thick. But this old bloke he was a rotten old swine. I am not kidding. But by God he made you work. You were no good to him unless you worked. What he

taught me when I went on the coal face did me a world of good. I was a ready made collier."

In 1918, when he was sixteen years of age, Mr. Instone found himself working with the 'iron man'.

"And I'll never forget him. The first shift I went on, afternoon shift quarter to three till quarter to ten. And I'd been loading the coal onto tubs. And he was rubbing the coal off his back. They used to be stripped to the waist and he stretched his arms and said,' Phew. Me tired's come.' And I said I'm afraid mine's come as well."

And on another occasion Mr. Instone learned how to keep his nerve:

"We were trying to break through to another district and the gate end came in. And we were trapped in there. There were three of us. I remember one chap. He was a bit scared, very much so and he didn't know what we were going to do so the other bloke – this chap from Arnold – 'Well' he said, 'you can please yourself. I'm going to eat my snap.' So I had to take my lead from him. Eventually they managed to get a road through to us but we were there about twelve hours."

During the 1921 coal strike, a group of Hucknall women played a football match with the Bulwell Belles to raise money for the miners' soup kitchen (photo: Hucknall Dispatch)

"You can please yourself. I'm going to eat my snap."

14   Nottinghamshire Miners' Tales

PART TWO: Life at the top

Keeping Clean
'Don't wash your back.'

The black faced miner, his clothes thick with pit dirt, has become a powerful symbol of the old mining industry. In the early days keeping clean was a real problem. Bob Foster, who was born in 1893 at Lambley recalls:

" ....*There was a pump at the bottom of Green Lane and when the men used to come down together to work at the pit (Gedling) they used to bring the buckets down. Two buckets to hang on the railings and they'd take them full of water when they'd finished their day's work."*

Gil Kirkby, also of Lambley and Gedling:

"We got our water from a spring across the road. I used to carry 28 buckets on a Sunday night for Doris to wash. I'd fill copper and washtubs you know."

Water was precious so pit clothes, which were soaked in sweat, had to be dried in front of the fire every night and washed once a week, but even then they remained stiff with dust. Each evening Sid used to wash at the sink but:

"The old saying was if you wash your back every night you'll get a bad back. So you only washed it once a week, Friday nights when you had finished your work."

Madge (Sid's wife) describes the Friday ritual:

"We used to have a gas geyser in the kitchen and the tin bath outside, so you had to take it off the hook and take it in the kitchen and swill it around and make sure the water was in the bath and drag it into the living room."

Sid:

"Not every one had got one, a geyser, we were modern."

Madge:

"When we were children ..... we used to all have a bath and we used to nearly fall out which were going to get in next."

There are no prizes for guessing who went in last at Sid and Madge's, followed of course by the pit clothes.

Some people were not so particular. Gil Kirkby remembers one old miner at Gedling in the 1930s:

"We had one old man, he came from Sheffield. He were an old athlete, used to do a lot of running, and he says, 'Well you know your trouble here, you blokes,' he says, 'You're likely to have bad feet.' He says, 'You wash 'em too often.' He

Michael Lakin at 7 months. A prize-winning photograph submitted by his father, Joseph Lakin, of Bestwood Colliery (photo: 'Coal' magazine October 1950)

Nottinghamshire Miners' Tales

were a scruff. Put a new vest on and he wore it out before he took it off. Phew! And he had to go out every night dressed up in a dickie bow and evening dress, dancing in Nottingham."

Spanish 'flu
'They were dying like flies.'
Mr. Instone, who was also at Gedling, has vivid memories of 1918 when he was sixteen years old:
"I remember when we had the Spanish flu. They were dying like flies and they used to let us come out of the pit at three quarter time. There were six of us, all of a size. Strong as young bulls. If the body was less than a mile from the church you weren't allowed to have a hearse and they had to carry them to the church. We used to bury them by lamplight. We were allowed to come out at twelve o'clock you see and we got 7s 6d for every body we carried. That was to make up for a quarter of your shift."
During the same period he also became unwell:
"I remember going to the doctors with me mother and it was packed. Eventually the doctor came out to the door and he says, 'You can all go home and die now. All I've got left is Epsom Salts.'"

Spanish flu was a pandemic which killed 40 million people throughout the world. It might more accurately be called French flu because it started in an army base camp in Étaples in northern France. A million soldiers went through there and when the end of the war came in 1918 they returned home carrying the deadly virus with them.

The 1920s and the Strikes
'It was a glorious summer.... Nobody wanted any coal.'

The 1920s brought further problems, especially two major strikes. The first was in 1921.
Bob Foster, who worked at Gedling until 1957, speaking about 1921:
"The manager said there's no work only if you want a shovel to fill. There was about 20,000 tons on the floor. .... (They had to heave the coal from the floor over into the wagons.) Well the first day or two me mother had to pull me shirt off. I couldn't wash me. They used to send the lot to Belgium. Small coal. Half inch coal."

Mr Instone:
"1921 strike I can vividly remember that. It was a glorious summer, dead against us. Nobody wanted any coal and it gave the management the opportunity of selling all the old stock. All the rubbish and everything. There used to be huge stocks leading right up to Mapperley tip of this slack and stuff and they sold that off. That was the year Dempsey fought Carpentier and old Carpentier broke his thumb on him and that was the year I met the wife. It (the strike) was for money. We got the Samuel Award. That was three

shillings a day basic."

Another casualty of the strikes was the miners' coal allocation. Kenneth Poynter, born in 1904, remembers how some of the Eastwood miners coped. His recollections are included in 'A century remembered. Reminiscences of everyday life in the Eastwood Area.'

".... Quite a number of miners in the area decided to start 'outcropping' (a form of surface mining) in the fields at the bottom of the 'common gardens' or the allotments. (The Rollings family were the landowners and gave them permission.) The miners dug deep down until they reached the 'bastard' seams which were of very inferior quality. Nevertheless it was coal and the old people in the area were glad to use it."

They also decided to sink a shaft:

"Many of these shafts were sunk in a position to serve two or three streets in the immediate area…. The elderly people in Queen Street, where we lived, and several streets around had a plentiful supply."

Mr. Poynter had permission to deliver the coal in the Boy Scout 'trek cart' but his father did not allow him to accept money or gifts from the old people. 'Outcropping' on a much larger scale also took place during the 1926 General Strike.

Even though the General Strike started with massive support, other workers capitulated after nine days which left the miners on their own.

A banner sent from China in the 1920s showing solidarity with British miners (Archives Dept, Museum of Labour History)

Nottinghamshire Miners' Tales

Mr Instone:
"It wasn't a strike it was a lockout. The minimum wage was fourteen shillings a day and they locked us out until we'd go back for ten shillings and three pence. I was out seven months."
Gil Kirkby:
"We were away eighteen weeks at Gedling. And George Spencer was a union man and that's when Gedling broke away (from the Union) in the 1926 strike. Some of 'em were out 28 weeks up at Mansfield. In all 18 weeks we was off on strike in '26 I was never out of a job, digging gardens, helping farmers, hoeing, shingling, anything where there was a shilling to be earned I was there. There was no strike pay. After the strike finished we got about a month's strike pay. Six shillings a week I think it was."
In 1926 Sid was just ten years old:
"During the strike my older brother used to go on this forest where there were hundreds of rabbits. They used to go rabbiting with a ferret and they used to sell them, sixpence each, that's what they were. But you would never believe what our mother could keep us three lads and our Dad on. Nothing. And when I say nothing I mean nothing. Not a farthing did they have. After about three weeks they had union money which weren't nearly enough. What my mother did, there was a corner shop right against us and she went to that bloke and asked him if she could have bare essentials and she'd pay him after strike were done. And he agreed to it to several women in the street and he gave them food, not bread, nobody would buy a loaf because they used to make their own. And whatever you really needed. No fags or anything like that. Then my mother paid so much a week after the strike was over. The same with rent. No rent paid but a week and a half when they started every week. They were worse off then than when they were on strike."

The Spencer Union, or the Nottinghamshire and District Miners' Industrial Union as it was officially known, lasted until 1937. Its opponents described it as a 'company and gaffers outfit', while George Spencer, its founder, saw himself as a realist, because miners were already returning to work in their thousands when he negotiated for some to get their jobs back. It caused deep divisions in the Nottinghamshire coalfields but finally came to an end after a dispute at Harworth when the coal owners agreed to recognise the Nottinghamshire Miners' Association.

The Dukeries
'The quaint old world village of Blidworth.... has been polluted with Bolshevic talk.'
In *'Between Two Worlds'*, R. J. Waller describes reactions to the arrival of mining in the Dukeries between 1913 and 1939. For in the 1920s, seven new coalmines were sunk in the area which caused profound changes in the eastern part of the county. During the first decades of the 20th century, tens of

The half winding wheel at the entrance to Thoresby Colliery

McChrystal's Snuff advertising handout in the form of a football fixture list

Nottinghamshire Miners' Tales

thousands of acres of Nottinghamshire were unspoilt rolling countryside and were the country estates of the Duke of Portland at Welbeck Abbey, The Duke of Newcastle at Clumber, Lord Savile at Rufford Abbey and Earl Manvers at Thoresby Hall. Their lordships were not always well disposed towards the idea of mining under their land. Lord Manvers was adamant, as a letter from his agent written in 1913 reveals:

'Lord Manvers is more than ever determined to have nothing to do with developing coal in the Thoresby area. It would certainly involve his giving up living there if he did so.'

Local people were also of the same mind, and the Mansfield Reporter of 7th March 1924 sums up their attitude when talking about a new colliery at Blidworth:

'It was said that probably before the builders left the village they would erect 2,000 houses. That means an enormous change for the quaint old-world village of Blidworth.... Already the colliery workers have invaded the village and the undefiled air of the parish has been polluted with Bolshevic talk.'

But there were pressing economic arguments, both national and personal. There was still, in the 1920s, a healthy demand from abroad for Nottinghamshire coal and their lordships found the royalties very useful for paying off their growing tax bills. Lord Manvers, however, did not want the new colliery to be called Thoresby and suggested it should be known as Edwinstowe Colliery. Neither did he want to be aware of its presence and continued to object, even until the 1930s, to the smoke from the Steam Plant at Thoresby which was visible from his land. Local people also disliked the increases in rates, disruption of their rural lifestyle and, to crown it all, that the miners did not even buy from the old village shops but used those in their own colliery village.

So the pits opened and colliery villages, such as New Ollerton, were built. The houses, which had hot and cold running water and large gardens, were regarded as the best homes for miners in Britain. There was also a factory where the increasingly emancipated womenfolk could find employment. Sport was encouraged and the immaculate appearance of the village led to it being described as a model village. But it was far from idyllic. Company 'policemen' made sure everyone obeyed the rules and if you did not fit in, especially at the pit, then dismissal and eviction could follow. And in this situation, even your own relatives in the same village would be forbidden to help you. Also those recently widowed were given very little time to find new accommodation.

Pastimes
'The collier almost always has a hobby, a dog, a pigeon, some kind of flower.'

But perhaps the fears about the influx of miners were not entirely unfounded. In his memoir of Sherwood, G.A. Tomlinson writes:

'I once asked a gamekeeper what animal caused him the most worry. I was

thinking of stoats, weasels, foxes and their like. But he answered sourly 'miners'. I knew well enough what he meant, for a collier when he sets his mind to it is the most skilful of poachers.'

In 1903, F.J. Metcalfe, Rector of Killamarsh, Derbyshire, wrote:

'The collier almost always has a hobby, a dog, a pigeon, some kind of flower, as gilliflower or dahlias, a bike: a collier's hobby must be something that will bring competition. You never find colliers with a dead hobby, he must be able to say to his companions 'I bet thee I can win thee.'

Sid:

"I had these pigeons, my brother had got a couple of ferrets, ferrets of course were kept for rabbitting.... I had one whippet and two greyhounds but I didn't know they were greyhounds. But the whippet I used to race at Shirebrook and I raced him eighteen times and he won nine out of eighteen . . .anyway one day, there were a gang of youths in the street including myself about eleven of us and I says to them Kip – that was the kennel name – will win tomorrow at Shirebrook. "Do you think so Sid?" I said I know so. I said he's racing against greyhounds but they can't get a start on him on this sharp track.

"So they all went down and they backed him and he won at 8 to 1. Wonderful. I had half a crown on him because I was off work at the time with an accident and I had no money. But I won a few quid on him. He won them a fortune but not one of them offered me a shilling for a pound of meat – it was horse meat and we used to buy it from the pet shop and it had blue stuff on it so you couldn't eat it. Anyway, I thought when I put the dog away for the night I'll never race you again, not for other peoples benefit. He was ever such a good dog. No, I never raced him again. I kept him for catching rabbits and he kept us in food during the war."

'Santone,' winner of the Manchester Sporting Chronicle whippet trophy (photo: 'Coal' magazine October 1950)

Cable bolting the roof at Welbeck Colliery (photo: Martyn Pitt for UK Coal)

The Miners' Welfare
The setting up of the Miners' Welfare Committee in the 1920s (later, the Miners' Welfare Commission) created new opportunities for miners. In the Notts/Derbyshire area there were six scholarships available for miners or members of their families.

Fred Simpson:
"..... my scholarship was for art. ..... for two days a week. But previous to that I used to go to Shakespeare Street five nights a week because I'd already got a monthly ticket for £1.15s.3d to go to Nottingham on the train..... I used to do a lot of landscape painting locally round Berry Hill and farm cottages and Papplewick Church and Papplewick Dam and Annesley. There was the Bolsover Colliery Art Club (which) were the founder of the Mansfield Arts Club as it is today. The first meeting was an open meeting and a lot of people were disappointed because it didn't tek into account music. There was room you see to open something like that in Mansfield at the time. But pictures weren't fetching no money and you couldn't afford to have one framed anyway. When Nationalisation came in 1947 there was always miners rallies and things like that which called for a tremendous lot of activities as regards painting."

Somehow Fred also found time to play football, cricket and even tennis.

The miners also organised outings. A talented sportsman might find that football or cricket provided an escape route from mining, so there was a keen interest, especially in football, as one old miner said recently;

"Where two are gathered together in Mansfield it's either football or mining."

Gil Kirkby, born in 1907, started at Gedling pit in 1921.

"We had a chap come out of Yorkshire.... He got to be foreman. He were a nice chap. We were all interested in football you know and he said, 'What do you think Gil? Should we run a trip to Hampden Park to the English and Scottish?' We paid all winter. We went by train. Buses come and picked us up and took us to Loch Lomond and Reg Leafe from Nottingham, a cousin of mine, was the referee. He was the only Englishman that's refereed England and Scotland."

Another favourite pastime was the colliery band with its smart uniforms and regular competitions. The influx of Welsh miners led to the forming of a male voice choir connected with Summit Pit. Miners were also great collectors and it is unusual to visit a retired or ex-miner's home without seeing mining memorabilia such as commemorative plates, carved and china figures, lamps and brass checks.

The St. John's Ambulance
Mining and its dangers was never far from their minds and, in their off duty time, many colliers attended classes held by the St. John's Ambulance Brigade.

An old miner said:
"I trained in first aid (in 1922) and was in the St. John. I used to go voluntarily. I trained in the Welfare Hall at Newstead."

Almost forty years later Norman Beadle attended St. John's Ambulance classes as well:
"We also had St. John's Ambulance on Mondays and Fridays. We used to go there and learn all about basic first aid, artificial respiration, all about bandaging and it put you in good stead for what to expect underground. We used to go away also. It was the added bonus that at the start of the season you went to Rhyl Miners' Holiday Town and at the end of the season you went to Skegness Miners' Holiday Camp. But I was interested in first aid."'
The first aiders at the pit always carried a basic first aid kit with them, and in the 1920's there were 50 first aid men at Newstead for some 1,200 miners. And even here the competitive spirit of the miners was used to the full.

At the Area Finals
'You stupid b******.'
Norman:
"Every colliery used to have a firefighting team and a first aid team. We won the area finals sometime in 1961 that was held at Bentinck. I was in the first aid team. We was in isolation until it was our turn to go on stage…. And after months and months of training we went onto the stage (in front of a large audience) to be met by an incident whereby a bloke was laid on the stage with his legs pointing outwards towards the audience. He was covered in chock blocks representing a fallen roof that he'd been injured by. So we removed the rubble from the patient, moved the patient nearer to the front of the stage getting him away from the hole above so that he was not hurt by any more falling rocks and I noticed a lump on his thigh. He was moaning. I took his belt off and his battery, undid his trousers and gently eased his trousers down and all he kept saying to me was 'You stupid b******'
Having pulled his trousers down a little bit further, I was more concerned with the lump that was on his leg and I did not notice that the guy had got no underpants on and (to the approving roar of the audience) I gave him the 'full monty!"

But in the view of the old miners there was little by way of safety equipment in the early days and, according to Fred Simpson:
"They used to have frequent accidents and it was always panic stations. It's no good people thinking the legislation, though it was there, always being carried out the way it had to be done under nationalisation. There were very

few inspectors and in any case when they came they were always guests. They were always nice and welcome. The mine were always acquainted when they were coming."

PART THREE: Dealing with emergencies

Accidents
'For God's sake get me out.'

Gil Kirkby who worked at Gedling:
"I remember where a bank came in and there was one man trapped at the far end and there was another man trapped at this end and my brother and me, we dug round to him. We got him bared so far to his waist and we got hold of his belt. Right, ready, pull. And we pulled and his belt broke and he shot backwards and the door came down again; killed him. If his belt hadn't broken we should have got him out. But the other chap at the other end, they managed to tunnel in from the other end to him and his hair had gone white."

In 1947 Bill was at Rufford when there was a roof fall:
".... And then it settled. All quiet. Just a few lights shining, heads turning and somebody saying, 'Are you there George?' or 'Are you there Bill?' We're all saying 'Yes' and then we heard this voice saying, 'For God's sake get me out. Get me out for God's sake. Get me out.' So we crawled back to have a look and there's this chappie and he's buried. (They called for help which eventually arrived and in the meantime started to move the roof off the injured man). When it all started again and it just came and came. We had no option but to run away, else stay and get buried..... and when we came back there was a great hole and a great heap and he was underneath."

It was after this tragedy that Bill decided to leave the mines for good.

Mr. Instone also had an accident, but it took more than that to stop production.
"A tub jammed me against the face and I broke this collar bone at about 12 o'clock. Well you weren't allowed to come out of the pit. I mean you had to

Nottinghamshire Miners' Tales 25

wait till knocking off time.... Unless you'd got a broken leg or something like that. So I had to stop in the gate and mark tubs for them. Then I went a two mile walk (to the pit bottom) and this thing was dragging me down but you couldn't go to the doctor till surgery time. That was 6 o'clock."

Sid's Story
'This steel prop.... flew and hit my head and knocked me over three times.'

It was with good reason that the old miners had a saying *'Keep your timber up'*, because one miner's carelessness could have terrible consequences for another. Sid's accident happened in the early years of World War II when he and his gang were setting steel props into position.

"... and one of them flew out. That was carelessness on another man who had set it to hold the roof up and he hadn't put what you called a lid on it.. You had to put a lid between the prop and the bar because if you didn't they would fly when the weight came on. They shouted for me to attend to another prop next to it which had a piece of muck hanging down. I was chargeman so it was my job to sort these things out. So I went up and I said there's a bit of muck here look, pulled it down and it hit this steel prop and it flew and hit my head and knocked me over three times. How it didn't break my neck I don't know, but it did a lot of damage. ..... I was bruised all down my throat, I couldn't eat for three weeks. I was in a state. I struggled to go to work. I had to for a week or two then pack up because of headaches."

Sid and Madge Radford

"It flew and hit my head and knocked me over three times."

No one ever accused Sid of malingering, but even experts could find nothing wrong with him. In desperation, a couple of years after the accident, Madge

26   Nottinghamshire Miners' Tales

sought help:

"We had to bring up two children on 30 bob a week. So I went and told him (the personnel officer at work) about how ill my husband was and I had to go out to work and I had two children. And I said the Duchess of Portland looks after miners when they are in difficulty. I would like you to write to her for me. And when she got the letter she came over on the Saturday morning and looked at him."

Over fifty years later, Madge and Sid still recall vividly how they felt when the Duchess turned up at their humble home in her chauffeur driven car and treated them so kindly and courteously.

The Duchess arranged for Sid to see Professor Pennycombe at Oxford, but it was local friends who collected the eight pounds to pay their train fare and expenses:

Sid:
"I had thirteen X-rays and this Pennycombe had got twelve trainees with him and I was naked on the bed and they were tapping this bone and tapping the other bone."

But when the Duchess returned to see them two weeks later she explained that the consultant, who even attended to the King, could only suggest migraine. It was an old friend who encouraged Sid to go to see Mary Green at Kirkby and gave them the fourpence each way bus fare to get there.

"I sat down on an ordinary chair back to front with my hands on the back. She never touched me she just looked at me and said, 'It's no wonder you've got headaches. You have got clots of blood on your spine and all the ligaments are off your scalp. Do you know anyone who works for the brewery?' I had two friends who did. 'Tell them to bring you some hops and put them in two muslin bags and warm them up in a steamer.' When one got hot I got it on my neck and when that had got cool, took if off and put the other one on for one and a half hours, two or three times a day. And that's what started to soften my neck."

1930s portrait of Winifred, 6th Duchess of Portland (Notts Local Library collection)

Madge:

"After a while, after he had gone two or three times he had got all bruises at the back of his neck and that bruise came out after all that while (two years) and tiny lumps just like peas. You could feel them."

Sid went to see Mary Green four times in all but she refused to accept any payment from him though she did take a handbag which Sid made for her. Sid made a full recovery, and he and Madge went on to develop a very successful window cleaning round in Mansfield.

Two Remarkable Women
helped Sid. The first was Winifred, 6th Duchess of Portland. Her obituary in the *Guardian Journal* of July 3rd 1954 echoes the sentiments which Sid and Madge expressed:

'Always considerate for the miners' welfare, especially those who had been injured while following their calling, she moved among them freely in their social and recreational centres.

In 1935, in recognition of her work among the people she was made a Dame of the British Empire.

Behind the honour was a very human story. Unknown to either the Duke or the Duchess, the secretary of the Notts Miners' Welfare Association, on behalf of the miners, their wives and their children, petitioned the King that some honour might be given to 'that angel, our beloved Duchess.'

The Green Memorial at Hucknall in its original town centre location, seen here on a c.1906 postcard

Apart from helping individual miners, she was also instrumental in setting up Harlow Wood Hospital and Portland Training College for the Disabled.

The other lady was Mary Green of Hucknall. The Greens were an exceptional family, five members of whom devoted their lives to healing. It is a story which goes back to Richard Green, who fought in France during the Napoleonic Wars in 1814, and spans more then 160 years. The most famous was Zacchariah, Richard's son, who compiled his own recipe book of herbal remedies.

In his monograph about the Green family, County Councillor Eric Morley, explains how, after 'Zachy's' death in 1898, a memorial was erected.

'It was built of granite .... and the cost, £400, was defrayed by public subscription. It stood originally at the junction of South Street, Baker Street and High Street but was removed to Titchfield Park.'

Mary Green was Zacchariah's grandaughter and *'it is estimated that in the space of 65 years her consultations greatly exceeded a quarter of a million.... When people returned to thank her, or sent letters of appreciation, she would say: 'Not me .... But God working through me.'*

After Mary's death those words were included in a tribute to her which was added to the memorial in 1982. The memorial still stands in Titchfield Park at Hucknall.

The Mines Rescue Service
or the Permanent Corps Rescue Brigade, as it was first known, was set up in 1906. There were so many accidents that the aim was to have properly trained men at each pit. These men were experienced miners who had already shown an interest in first aid by being members of the St John's Ambulance Brigade.

Stan Stanton was a member of one of the teams at Cotgrave until the pit closed:

"It was voluntary really. All you got paid for it was about £200 a year so you didn't do it for the money."

'My father, Mr J. G. Huskisson, who died ten years ago at the age of 86 was the first Chief Instructor at your station in 1909'

By 1912 it became compulsory for pits to have several trained teams of rescue workers so that each shift was covered. They were first on the scene when an accident occurred, and had to attend regular training sessions at their local Miners' Rescue Station under the supervision of the permanent members of the brigade who were based there. At one time there were 25 stations across the country, of which only four remain, including the one on Leeming Lane at Mansfield Woodhouse. Full time members were recruited from those already involved in rescue work at their own pit. In 1961 the chief instructor at Mansfield received a letter from V. G. Huskisson:

'Dear Sir,
No doubt your assistant instructor informed you of my visit to your station last

month, when I promised to send you photos of 50 years ago.

My father, Mr. J. G. Huskisson, who died ten years ago at the age of 86 was the first Chief Instructor at your station in 1909, and the house next door was built for him.

I was indeed sorry to see that the old station was no longer in use, as it was my intention to ask your permission to have a look over it and so recall the happy days I spent, when then only eight years of age.

Regarding the enclosed photos, each team from different pits had their photos taken. No doubt very few of these men would be alive today as 50 years is going back some time, but it is possible that some of their sons may be passing through your hands, in which case they would be very interested.'

Gedling Colliery no. 1 rescue team, pictured at Mansfield Rescue Station in 1911 with J.G. Huskisson, the first chief instructor

The Rescue Station moved to its present premises in 1958 where the new underground galleries could reproduce even more closely the smoke-filled and humid conditions of a typical mining accident.

"Each team from different pits had their photos taken."

Joining the Brigade
'What the hell do you think you're doing?'
Norman Beadle joined the Rescue Brigade in the late 1960s ;
"They were tied houses with the job. We moved from Blackwell on the Monday morning into a very large house on Leeming Lane South, which was a massive house compared to the two up two down outside bath on the wall. We had more space than we had furniture at that particular time."
There was, as usual, an initiation for the new boy.
"Friday morning at the Rescue Station used to be scrub day where everything was hosed down, brass was brassoed, all the apparatus was cleaned, tested. Monday to Thursday was kept for training days for the part time rescue men. My first week I was delegated to hose the garage down and scrub all the floor, clean the vehicles etc., along with another bloke. Also on Friday mornings we cleaned the manager's car. What I didn't know was he had gone on a conference or something like that and he wasn't there for the week. I was told I had to clean the manager's car. I said you're joking but they said 'No. We clean the manager's car.' But I didn't realise that one of the lads put **his** car in the manager's dock. So I gets a bucket of soapy water and there was this beat up old car which I duly started to clean thinking to myself that this manager couldn't have much money or he was a mean so and so, only to be met by an officer name of G. A. T. Burton and he says, 'What the hell do you think you are doing?' I said cleaning the manager's car. He said, 'That's not the bloody manager's car. It's your bloody mate's car."
Norman soon discovered that there many opportunities to better yourself by getting your officer's ticket.
"You had to get a shot firer's ticket, get your deputy's ticket, you had to be face trained. There was like a three year course on rescue work, gas inhalations, explosions, spontaneous combustion. Everything appertaining to rescue work, legislation was covered on this course and at the end of it you sat two 3 hour papers and a practical which was in three parts which was legislation, apparatus and gallery. The hardest exam was the gallery under the station because you didn't know what was going to happen."
Norman did all his revision confident in the knowledge that legislation was his best subject:
"I thought I'd cracked it. Cocky. And I went in and did my three questions and looked and looked at these three questions, and I was allowed three minutes to study them and 15 minutes to answer them. And I was still looking at them 18 minutes later. My mind just went blank. I couldn't think of a thing. And I had to go 6 months later to retake. And I walked in, looked at the questions and I said I'm ready and I walked out of there in under three minutes. I'd answered the questions and got my officer's ticket."

"So I gets a bucket of soapy water and cleans this beat up old car."

Summoned by Bells

But there were certain disadvantages to the job:

"*What hurt more than anything was a lovely summer's evening if you were awaiting duty, you couldn't go out. You'd sit on the wall at the top and watch people go by with their families. It was the same for the ladies. If one of the women wanted to go shopping she had to take all the children with her down Mansfield because she couldn't leave them alone with her husband unless another lady would fetch them in and look after them if the bell went.*"

All the men lived in tied houses which were within half a mile of the station. Upstairs on the wall on the landing or the main bedroom was the bell which was rung at the station, calling them in an emergency but which could not be switched off at the house.

Jean, Norman's wife:

"*One night I had to go up to the night watchman and said turn the bells off because they were still going. He'd not realised to turn it off. The bells would ring in all the houses.*"

But Jean does remember some good times:

"*Then there were the dances and everything. It was always a long dress. You couldn't wear a short dress could you? The ladies wore long dresses. In fact I've still got some upstairs.*"

There was a snooker team which took part in the Wynne Billiard Shield, the prizes for which, in 1941 were, according to the rule book:

'*25 shillings (first) 15 shillings (second) and 10 shillings (third). The players winning the inter station play will also receive an additional prize to the value of 10 shillings.*'

Emergency at Doe Lea

'**We all looked at one another and felt as though we'd failed. The first one with black damp and everything was blue.**'

Norman:

"*The first time I was involved in an emergency I can always remember it. It was a lovely summer afternoon and then the station bells went at about twenty past three and we all ran. And at that time of the day you had all your pit clothes on the vehicle itself on the racks at the top. You had to get changed on the vehicle heading towards the incident. The incident was at Doe Lea colliery. Two men had been overcome by black damp gas. A third man who had gone to have a look for them had also been affected by this black damp, which is basically lack of oxygen and he was in a bit of a stupor. Doe Lea was a small private (drift) mine near the motorway which goes up towards Chesterfield. With it being a private mine very little attention was paid to safety. The conditions were terrible.*"

Water came through Doe Lea from Glapwell Pit and the level had to be checked regularly by monitoring a box which was in a ditch.

"*As he bent down to close the box of course he got a whiff of black damp, no oxygen, he went down straight away. But the bloke that was with him, - this is*

all we can surmise – must have thought he had a heart attack or something like that and he jumped in after him to try and get him out and when his head went down into it, lack of oxygen hits quickly, everything stops and you're down....
We got them out into fresh air. We knew it was fresh air because we had a candle so we had got at least 18% oxygen and we'd got a canary. If the bird was still tweeting about on its perch, he was alive so you were alive."

They put an oxygen reviver on the patient and gave artificial respiration, even breaking the patient's ribs in the process but after nearly two hours they had to give up.

"We all looked at one another and felt as though we'd failed. The first one with black damp and everything was blue."

Canaries
Canaries were used for detecting gas until the 1990s.

Mansfield Rescue Station, like most collieries, had its own aviary, and the team always took two birds with them on call out. The canaries were well cared for and even had their own breathing apparatus officially known as a 'humane chamber'. Nowadays, electronic devices have replaced the birds.

The humane chamber

The Nottinghamshire coalfields were comparatively safe and few disasters occurred, so those involved in rescue work often found themselves helping at

Checking for gas on the coalface at Thoresby (photo: Martyn Pitt for UK Coal)

pits which were in Derbyshire or South Yorkshire. Also, certain pits on the borders of Nottinghamshire were usually regarded as part of the Nottinghamshire coalfields.

The Markham Disaster

All safety measures were in place at Markham and the correct procedures were followed, but even so disaster struck, resulting in 18 deaths and 12 serious injuries.

The official report states:

'At about 5.35 a.m. on Monday 30th July 1973, the day shift winding engine man, R.W. Kennan, arrived at No. 3 winding engine house as the last of the night shift men were being wound to the surface. Some 20 minutes later Kennan operated the winding engine to wind the first dayshift men into the mine, and by about 6.20 a.m. 105 persons had been lowered.

The overlap rope cage was then loaded at the surface with 15 men on the top deck and 14 on the bottom deck. The wind proceeded normally until the cages had passed the mid point in the shaft, when Kennan began to retard the engine and, out of the corner of his eye, saw "some sparks under the brake cylinder" and heard a bang. He immediately moved the control lever towards the "off" position to increase regenerating braking and simultaneously pulled the brake lever towards the "on" position. Operation of the brake lever felt "the same as picking up a pen" and had no effect on the speed of the winding engine drum. Kennan continued moving the control lever towards the "off" position, but it appeared to him that this had little effect on the drum speed so he pressed the emergency stop button. He expected to see the drum "brought to a sudden stop" but nothing happened and, as a last resort, he switched off the motor for the hydraulic pump which supplied the "ungabbing" gear. This had no effect on the winding engine and the next thing Kennan remembered was bricks falling around him.

Damaged cage in the pit bottom at Markham (HMSO)

Winding engine house damage at Markham (HMSO)

'The ascending cage was detached from the underlap rope by the operation of the detaching hook in the headframe bell, but continued to ascend until it struck the roof girders of the airlock structure, where it fractured the surrounding concrete and brickwork. As there were no safety catches in the headframe, the cage then dropped back until it was hanging by its suspension chains from the detaching hook.

'The descending cage carrying the men crashed into the pit bottom with such force that it fractured 9 of the 17 wooden landing baulks. Although power had been cut off before the crash, the momentum of the winding system unwound the spare coils of overlap rope and then the sword capel (a metal unit into which the end of the rope was embedded), with part of the drum side and brake path, was torn away. The rope and capel were pulled over the headgear pulley and then fell down the shaft on top of and alongside the cage containing the men. The drum continued to rotate, and the flailing capel of the underlap rope seriously damaged the winding engine house and an adjoining workshop.'

Adam McFee, who retired from the Mines Rescue at Mansfield in 1988, remembers:

"We got an early morning call. We had to take the emergency winder to Markham. The Chesterfield team were already underground helping to take *out the dead and injured. When we got to Markham it was chaos at the pit top. There was damage to the cage and headstocks and there were reporters and TV crews all over the place."*

The mobile emergency engine wound a "hoppit" (a small cage capable of carrying one or two men) so that the shaft could be inspected, and then the cage had to be raised. The lower deck was *"severely distorted,"* but there was little damage to the top deck.

Adam:

"Before we could bring it up, special links had to be made to match those on the cage. We had a 5 ton lift winder so the cage had to be made lighter. It took almost a week and when it came up the bottom of the cage was like that. (cups his hands together)."

There are only six emergency winders in the country. Allan Platt is in charge of the one at Mansfield and travels the country servicing the others and conducting trials at every mine which has a shaft. One recent job was at a large potash mine in the north east.

Overwinding occurred when the braking system failed and the cage travelled too far into the headstocks. Early in the twentieth century, various measures were introduced to prevent this. The height of the headstocks was raised and braking systems were installed. However, a special detaching hook was fitted, so that if all else failed, a cage which overshot entered a bell-shaped hook which unfastened the rope but held on to the cage. The one most commonly used in Nottinghamshire was invented in 1866 by John King of Pinxton and known as King's Patent. If a cage overshot, it was described as having "Kinged". These detaching hooks were still in use in the 1970s alongside the modern electronic monitoring.

Explosion at Thurcroft

In *'Pit Talk – Memories of Manton'*, compiled by David Hopkins, Barry Harris recalls:

'I was accepted in the rescue team in 1964 and one of the worst incidents was a gas explosion at Thurcroft Colliery (S. Yorkshire) The explosion was on a new coalface and four tailgate rippers had been killed. The area was on fire when we got there, so we had to put a sandbag stopping on both the loader gate and tailgate....

It took three weeks for the fire to go out, we then returned to Thurcroft. I was captain of the No.1 team and it was our job to locate and mark the position of the bodies on a map. The scene was of total devastation, the Eimco machine and the remotes (electrical equipment) had been blown back 50 or 60 yards from the rip and all the rings (roof supports) had been blown out. We found two bodies but by then we had to withdraw as our time had run out. We were then replaced by No2 team who carried on with the search. They found the other bodies. The only way they could be identified was by their brass tallies or the number plate on the back of their lamp battery.'

Bringing out the Injured
Dealing with an injured man underground presented enormous problems. Just getting a man off the coalface could take more than half an hour. Tony Whelan's book *'Send for t'oss'* contains some vivid description:
'The carrying of the stretcher was always the biggest problem. It may have been necessary to clear a belt of coal so we could drag a man down on a Neil-Robertson stretcher. You may well have to wait until supports are taken out because you couldn't bend a rigid stretcher round props. Because of the delays there was a lot of miners die who would have lived, but died two or three days later because of shock. Prior to nationalisation (there was also a problem with the cage) you couldn't lay a stretcher down. So we had to use a Lowmoor jacket and we had to 'walk' him on.... He was supported by this jacket at an angle on the side of the cage and then one man could travel with him.'

1950s rescue team. Their equipment includes a canary cage

A nurse who was experienced in treating miners during the 1930's remembers:
'There was one ambulance which brought them in which was very shaky. It was a wonder they didn't die before they got to hospital....The ambulance driver was called Joe and I think it was a case of 'waiting for Joe' from one place to another.... The miners were absolutely super but they were brought in often severely shocked'
After 1944, first aid teams were allowed to administer morphine, which saved many lives. However, there might still be a wait before reaching hospital, especially if the ambulance served more than one pit. On one occasion they had to wait for the ambulance from the Mansfield Rescue Station, but when it arrived a great deal of equipment, including bird cages, had to be removed.

Nottinghamshire Miners' Tales

PART FOUR: The war years and after

The Thirties
'.... Miners' children running about without any shoes or stockings because they couldn't afford to dress them properly.'

In the 1930s, the coal industry was in crisis and to avoid closures the government imposed a quota system so that mines were only open for a short time each week. Harold Henshaw, who was born in 1894, was interviewed at Arnold in 1984. In the 1930s he was working for the Mines Safety Research Board:

'I was shocked to see the conditions of the workmen. It was in the 1930s when the pits were working about half a day a week and the miners used to sit you know on the side of the roadway having their snap. And as I was going past they'd open the 'bait tin' as they used to call it and say, 'Look this is my snap today.' Dry bread or bread and dripping and they'd tell me stories about their children and of course I used to see it in the streets .... miners' children running about without any shoes or stockings because they couldn't afford to dress them properly.'

In the 1920s Harold was in mine management in Nottinghamshire:

'You see that was in the days of private enterprise. The owners were dictatorial and they were saying to me as a manager, 'Look you must cut that work they are doing there, instead of giving them 10 shillings a yard give them nine.' Remember all management officials were themselves employees so had great sympathy for the miners.'

Towards the end of the 1930s, because of the threat of war, rearmament started, which meant there was more demand for coal. Also, it was assumed that our main export market, France, would require large quantities of coal. But the fall of France in 1940 meant that Britain was left with large stocks.

The Home Guard
'What a motley lot we were.'

At the outbreak of war, some miners were allowed to join up, but not Bill, who remained in the pit and had to join the Home Guard instead:

'.... What a motley lot we were. I was made a platoon commander. We had a regular sergeant teaching us but unfortunately we only had brush handles 'cos there were no rifles. We had a rifle to share between us for learning to train with and clean but we had to use the brush handles for drill. And then we used to march along there very proud in these baggy Home Guard uniforms that didn't fit any of us and march up onto the Forest with the rifle, passing it round. And we'd have hand grenades which we were always taught to count ten and nobody managed to survive that long. We were

throwing them before we got the pin out nearly.
There was also air raid warden duty:
'Twice a week minimum, at the highest point in Mansfield, Berry Hill near the Miners' Rehabilitation Centre.'

Dunkirk

The fall of France in the summer of 1940 led to the evacuation of thousands of British troops from Dunkirk in northern France:

"After Dunkirk they brought in lots and lots of trainloads of wounded into this area in the Mansfield Central Goods Yard....(It was August/September and the schools were used as billets). I had a flair for the mouth organ and I used to go into the school at night and join these Tommies. And they were wounded and that and we'd sit round in gangs and I'd play the harmonica and they'd all have a sing song with it. That's just a small part of your daily routine after your work."

There were also fears that the headstocks would be bombed and create chaos underground. One old miner recalls:

"The first day the war started I were detailed for a job to go through some old workings to couple Bilsthorpe up with Rufford. They all got coupled up didn't they, underground, Clipstone, Crowny, Sherwood. They were all coupled up for if there were any war activity and they knocked the headstocks down, they could get out."

Another remembers:

"I were stood on Sherwood pit top waiting to go down the pit when the bombers started to go to Sheffield. They seemed to be only just above the headstock. I were stood on the pit top and I watched them start dropping bombs and the ack ack guns going. We stood as long as we dared."

Careless Talk

The county was preparing itself for war – at first referred to as the emergency - as entries in the handwritten Record Book of Mansfield Rescue Station show:

' A. R. P. Instruction No.1.

When warning by telephone is given regarding air raids the following procedure must be adopted:

Red Warning. For men at home intermittent short rings on the call bells are to be given by the duty men for about 15 minutes following which all men must report at once to the duty room. (Men must not run to the duty room on these occasions) After reporting they may be required to stand by at the station or at home at the discretion of the Superintendent.

Red Warning. All men standing by should assemble in the duty room to receive instruction for getting ready to turn out on receipt of an emergency call.

All leave men should return to the station as soon as possible when public air raid warnings are given.

Green Warning. The brigade will stand by at the discretion of the Superintendent.
White Warning. Normal operations will operate.
Mansfield 25th August 1939   Signed G. L. Brown Manager.'

However in September a stern reminder was issued:
'To Recipients on the 'Special' Air Raid Warning List:
It has come to notice that in some parts of the country recipients of the Preliminary Caution (Air Raid Message Yellow) and those who have been officially informed of the receipt of this message, have passed on the information to persons other than those to whom they must make it known in the course of their official duties. Information thus given has spread in the district affected with the result that the general public have assumed that an air raid was imminent.
I therefore wish to impress on all recipients of the Preliminary Caution in the County of Nottingham and all those that are authorized to become aware of it that this message is strictly confidential and that special care should be exercised to ensure that the knowledge of its receipt is not communicated to any person to whom it should not be known.
Shire Hall Nottingham 22nd Sept 1939   F. T. Lemon Lieut. Colonel
                                                Chief Constable

Air Raids

The worst year for air raids in Nottinghamshire was 1941 when there were thirteen raids between January and July. These are listed by John Hook in *'But All Are Losers. The Air Raids on Nottinghamshire 1940 – 1941.'* The most devastating occurred on three consecutive nights, Thursday, Friday and Saturday, May 8th, 9th and 10th when the city was the main target. Most fatalities were on the first night when 48 perished in the Co-operative Bakery on Meadow Lane and there were many other casualties across the city. A memorial to the victims of the Bakery incident was erected at Wilford Hill Cemetery. But the mines were not damaged.

'Coming home on a wing and a prayer.'
Councillor Fred Riddell started work at the Bottom Pit near Hucknall in 1940 and recalls the war in Peter Housden's book, *'Local Statesmen'*
Councillor Riddell:
"We were lucky, there were hardly ever air raids. We used not to bother to go down into the air raid shelters.... When I was on night shift at the pit, I used to take the dog for a walk before breakfast and would see the bombers coming back from their night bombing raids piloted by the Poles (stationed at Hucknall Aerodrome). Quite literally you could sometimes see through them.... You could see the hits on them and the holes in the fuselage. There used to be a song that was very popular at the time. Those Poles were all Catholics 'Coming home on a wing and a prayer.' I had a tremendous respect

for them which has never left me."
The Polish airmen earned the admiration and gratitude of local people and a number of Poles joined the mining industry after the war.

The only incident in Hucknall which John Hook records happened in 1940, when an allied plane crashed into a house in Hucknall, tragically killing all the occupants. But the ever present threat of air attacks brought the war very close to home.

Miners were generous supporters of the *Wings for Britain* campaign and raised money for urgently needed Spitfires, both by levies and voluntary contributions.

Shortages

It seemed to the miners that they now worked very long hours and sometimes did double shifts. Shortage of materials caused many problems.
Bill:
"Our biggest trouble was getting trucks from the railway because there was always a shortage what with the bombings of the railway. And see if you couldn't get the trucks it meant stopping the colliery 'cos there was nowhere to put the coal in those days. Today they'd bulldoze it away. Didn't go home. You waited for some trucks coming. Used to be ringing all over the country for trucks."

Neal Kirk, who was a Bevin Boy (see below) in 1944, remembers one of the jobs he had to do at Gedling:

IN THE HOUR OF PERIL
MINERS OF
NOTTINGHAMSHIRE AND
DISTRICT
EARNED THE GRATITUDE
OF THE BRITISH NATIONS
SUSTAINING THE VALOUR OF
THE ROYAL AIR FORCE
AND FORTIFYING THE CAUSE
OF FREEDOM
BY THE GIFT OF
SPITFIRE AIRCRAFT
They shall mount up with wings as eagles
Issued by the Ministry of Aircraft Production
1942

Plaque commemorating the Spitfire fund

"I was attached to Joe Upton to help him draw off the steel girders from old disused roadways for recycling. That was a very dirty job, drawing old districts off. Districts that hadn't been used for years and years. They found there was a shortage of steel which they wanted to get out and recycle.
Then came my first shock. Normally the roads were semi-circular but these over the years with the weight upon them had become like a Λ shape. You had to crawl through this to start off with. We pulled them out with a winch and when they fell the clouds of old coal dust was unbelievable. I went down the pit white and came up absolutely black. The showers were a godsend....
It was a case of lots of scrubbing to remove the ingrained coal dust. To get your eye lids clean and coal dust free was almost impossible."

Jo Upton, with whom Neal worked, was very respected by the other miners and was organist at Lambley Methodist Church. Many of the older miners were regular attenders at their local church or chapel and often tee total. But others enjoyed a pint after work, especially on a Friday night at 'The Welfare' and there was quite a competition to be first out of the showers and into the bar. In wartime there was a tendency to over-indulge when beer was available, to make up for the occasional shortages.

Bevin Boys
'You're warm. You'll do.'
'Bevin Boys' was the nickname given during World War II to the young men who, once they were eligible for service in the armed forces, were instead drafted into the mining industry. The system was devised by Ernest Bevin who was the wartime Minister for Labour and National Service. The role of these young men and their contribution to the war effort has often been undervalued and misunderstood, possibly because the criteria by which they were selected changed as the war progressed.

Before 1941 some miners were allowed to 'join up' and some were even 'called up'. But this created a shortage of miners, so mining became a reserved occupation and up till 1943 conscripts were given the choice of working down the mines, for they had to work underground, or serving in the armed forces. These were known as optants or volunteers and numbered over 23,000. But there was still a shortfall, and towards the end of the war many young men between the ages of 18 and 25 were informed that their *'number had come up'*. In other words the final digit of their National Service number had been selected and they were not required for the armed forces but for work in the pits. They had no choice in the matter and served under the same rules as if they had been in the forces.

Somehow the idea took root that the Bevin Boy was *'placed into the coal mining industry because of his convictions as a conscientious objector.'* But in his book *'The Forgotten Conscript. A History of the Bevin Boy.'* Warwick Taylor points out that "*Facts show that there were 41 (conscientious objectors) out of a total of 47,859 Bevin Boys.*" He goes on to describe the caution and sometimes resentment which they initially encountered from the miners. Though once the boys showed themselves willing to work they experienced the usual

"Your number's up" - a cartoon by Lee published in the London Evening News in January 1944

generous good humour from the mining community. However, they still had to endure the disapproval of the general public and were constantly having their papers checked by the police, just to make sure that they were not deserters.

Many Bevin Boys who worked in Nottinghamshire were from down south and lived in either hostels or digs. One old lady from Mansfield remembers:

"Because I couldn't go to work because I had got youngsters, I had Bevin Boys. I had one from London and one from Aylesbury, and they were grand lads. They really were nice lads. One, his father was on the railway in a reserved occupation, and he was a gardener and he used to send us boxfuls of garden vegetables up when Leslie used to go home for the weekend."

There were hostels at Eastwood, Hucknall, Mansfield East, Mansfield North and Worksop. Several others were set up but not actually used. Warwick Taylor describes the pros and cons of hostel and private accommodation:

'Hostels provided …. regular meals and snacks, hot showers, recreational facilities and medical treatment, whereas …. in the private house, many of which were miners' small terraced houses which were invariably spotless …. one could enjoy good home cooking and often be treated as one of the family. If there were not pit head baths available at the colliery, it would mean taking a hot bath in the tin bath in front of a roaring fire. The fire was usually kept going throughout the year for this purpose, coal being provided free to the household of married miners. The only other inconvenience would be to trek down to the end of the garden in order to use the toilet, no joke on a cold winter's night.'

Neal Kirk, who was 18 in July 1944, really wanted to join the airforce but was turned down along with the 50 others who were interviewed in Birmingham at the same time. By September, he was studying Chemistry at Nottingham University College when he received instructions to go to Cresswell Colliery on December 28th to complete a month's training. This came as quite a shock to a lad who had attended public school and had a sheltered and privileged existence. However, at the end of January 1945, Neal presented himself at Gedling pit which was only two miles from his home:

"The first thing I remember was the visit to the pit doctor. He was housed in a little old building on the other side of the sidings. He tested my chest, took my temperature, said 'You're warm. You'll do.' And so I was accepted as a miner."

Neal was issued with a key to a locker and a lamp check number -117- *"never to be forgotten."* The lamp was heavy and usually carried on a belt. What Neal longed for was a cap lamp.

Ponies were still very much in evidence:

"There were about six ponies working down the pit and they were extremely well looked after – plenty of food, warmth, clean stables and a very caring ostler. He gave me Craig, a quiet 25 year old Shetland pony..... I hitched him onto a tub of materials to be taken down the roads and said go on. Then gee

up. And he never moved. I asked a nearby miner how to get him started and he said 'Move you **** **** *****' and away Craig went."

Warwick Taylor:

"The pony was a very useful friend in the event of a faulty miners' lamp, when the animal would by instinct lead the way back to the pit bottom in total darkness."

But Neal did not feel like a real miner until:

"Two of us were given the job of back packing behind the coal face …. The weight had come down and the 3 foot height had been reduced to 1 foot 3 inches and we had to crawl in on our stomachs to extract the valuable steel props. This was done by winch and hammers. We had been given cap lamps. Now we were men! I clearly remember the deputy coming along the road and asking if we were alright. I said yes but it's a bit tight. His reply was 'Keep your mind off women and you won't be trapped.'"

Occasionally Bevin Boys were asked to work at the coal face and clear an absent miner's stint:

"A stint for a miner was 9 yards but a Bevin Boy had a maximum of 7 yards, so two of us had to do it. And it was very hard work; non-stop because the stint had to be cleared to let the cutter through ready for the next shift."

It was because the miners did such exhausting physical work that they were awarded extra food rations, some of which could be enjoyed in better meals in the canteen. Neal was certainly fit after working underground:

"If the wheels of a full tub came off the rails I could lift it back on. The tubs weighed three quarters of a ton fully laden."

His most interesting job was working on a new heading (tunnel) for the first man-ride train in Gedling:

"When a tunnel is being made air cannot go in naturally. It had to be blown in as we progressed. Unfortunately we had to take our air from the hot return airway so the conditions were unpleasant but the money was better. There were three of us in the team, the boss being Cecil Saxton, a well-built man who at the weekend downed many, many pints of beer. We worked in shorts and helmet only and on a Monday, within five minutes, pints of liquid came pouring out of Cecil! He was a man full of humour, like many of the miners I worked with and it certainly helped."

Bevin Boys often hated the work but they were governed by strict rules and persistent absenteeism could be punished with a prison sentence. In fact no one was allowed to leave the mines until 1947. It was with very mixed feelings that Neal left in 1948:

"I had enjoyed the experience. Going down the pit a boy and leaving the pit a man – a wiser and stronger man. I have often reflected on my Bevin Boy days with a certain pride and gratitude for the opportunity of mixing with such a fine body of men."

Even though Bevin Boys were drafted down the pits

Neal Kirk

they never had those years of service added to their pensions like members of the armed forces and neither did they get a 'demob' suit. However, it was the training of the Bevin Boys which led to the proper training of future young entrants to the industry. In the year 2000 Bevin Boys were represented at the Cenotaph for the first time.

Years after leaving the mine, Neal was teaching maths at a secondary school:

"An irate parent wished to see me. He was six feet tall and at least 14 stone. I had given his boy a taste of my slipper. Now a jailable offence. The miner was originally from Durham, working at Cotgrave Pit. He thought all the people in West Bridgford looked down on the miners. What an unnecessary chip on his shoulder!

When the conversation started to get heated I pointed out that I knew one person in the room had worked at the coal face but I didn't know if two people had. He was shell shocked and stopped dead in his tracks. We chatted a long time about our mining experiences and his last words to me were 'If he upsets you again just belt him.' I never had any problems with any miners' children after that. Good news travels fast. My past saved me."

In 1945 there were 44 mines in Nottinghamshire employing a total of 45,587 men of whom 34,439 worked underground. The coalfield was successful and prosperous so that by the end of the war in 1945 many working class families found themselves better off because, in spite of the wartime dangers and hardships, they had enjoyed full employment for the longest period in decades. Compared with other groups, miners were quite well paid. Neal Kirk earned more as a Bevin Boy than he did four years later as a newly qualified teacher.

Nationalisation, at Last!
'Out of darkness cometh light.'

The Miners' Federation of Great Britain and the Labour Party were very much in favour of Nationalisation and pressing for it even during the war. So it was with great hopes for the future that they celebrated the setting up of the National Coal Board on 1st January 1947. Their original motto says it all: *'E Tenebris Lux – Out of Darkness Cometh Light.'*

Original logo of the National Coal Board

In 1947, when the country's 958 mines were nationalised, 700,000 men worked down the pit. There was a honeymoon period when millions of pounds were spent on improvements above and below ground. Rufford was typical in having deepened shafts and new headstocks and buildings above ground. Gone were the piles of rubble and ramshackle appearance so that some collieries actually produced publicity post cards!

PART FIVE: Mechanisation

Problems and Complaints
'The vicar's ringing up. The garden's full.'
Gradually the dreary business spent at the screens sorting out 'bat' as the coal was prepared for sale became highly technical and was replaced by coal preparation plants. Clean coal will float and can be skimmed off, but the water left in the tank is filthy and must not be let out. Bob Foster, who worked at Gedling, describes the consequences:

"One of the wash boxes was broken and even though you weren't supposed to let the water out eventually they had to. Well, the brook went through Gedling Vicarage and it was all that black stuff. The next day the manager said 'What went off last night? The vicar's ringing up. The garden's full.' Well I said, they had a breakdown and he had to let so much water out but I said we can get over that. I'll send a man or two down. 'Well,' he said 'I've had another rector on at me from Lambley. He's complaining about dust.' They'd just started that aerial ropeway (taking waste from the pit up onto the tip.) and when the wind was in the wrong direction it blew the dust."

But no one minded sorting that out because on this occasion it was mainly a group of young mini-skirted housewives who had to be visited.

The Old and the New

Meanwhile, things were changing rapidly at the coalface. In the old days coal was 'hand got'. Bill, who was at Rufford until 1947, explains:

"We used to have a blade that had a slot in it at the top and you used to put the pick blade into it …. And then you had a cotter that you drove in underneath it. Every night you had to take them blades out of the pit and have them sharpened and there used to be a man with a little forge on top and you used to pay him once a week for sharpening the blades. He used to tie them up in a bundle and drop them in at the blacksmith's shop when he'd finished…. They'd all be in the tub down at the pit bottom."

But greater use of electrical power underground meant that more efficient and powerful machinery could be introduced so, by 1945, a cutter loader had been developed which, as its name suggests, was able to cut the coal and load it onto a conveyor belt. The old miners thought these new machines amounted to slavery. Mr Instone remembers mechanisation at Gedling:

"…. They brought in a coal cutter. To start with we went in Thursday morning and we had to fit all these things together and make 'em work and it was Sunday afternoon when I came out of the pit next time. They used to send us bread and cheese down from Chase Farm.'

Mick Noble, who was at Mansfield Colliery between 1962 and 1977 and is now Deputy Superintendent at the Mines Rescue Station:

"When I was at Mansfield I used a machine called a trepanner at the coal

Harworth Colliery heading machine (photo: Martyn Pitt for UK Coal)

Coalface at Clipstone (photo: Martyn Pitt for UK Coal)

Nottinghamshire Miners' Tales

face to cut coal suitable for household use. In those days Mansfield had 8 working coal faces but in a modern pit it is 2 or 3 at most. Also, the old machines had to be serviced almost every week so Saturday was the day when one machine would go up for servicing and another would be brought down. Nowadays, machines last for as long as the coal face is being worked."

Paul Wilkinson – also at the Mines Rescue Station:

"I worked on the Yard seam (3 foot wide) at Sherwood. The machine I used was a shearer and it cut the coal smaller so that it was suitable for power stations. A shearer had to be taken underground in 3 or 4 sections and then rebuilt in the tail gate. (The roadway along which the stale air left the pit). I remember when we broke the European record for one week's production and we were treated to a free bar at the Welfare."

The Price of Progress

But although it increased production, mechanisation came at a price. Mr Instone again:

"I remember seeing one chap. He got his leg in a coal cutter and got his foot cut off.... We shoved a bit of bind at the back of his leg, tied it up together and stopped the bleeding and carted him out."

Bill:

".... One of the jibbers had dropped a prop right behind the cutter which is moving all the while but it jammed underneath, stopped and he'd dropped the prop on and the chain and the machine wasn't moving and this prop was pounding his face to bits."

Industrial Illnesses

Mining has always had its share of industrial illnesses, and there were also long term consequences from the noise, dust and vibration of the machinery. In a telephone conversation in March 2001, Mr Michael Stevens, General Secretary of the UDM, gave the following information:

"The most common industrial illnesses are:

Bronchitis and emphysema. There are 14,500 cases pending but it can take up to 8 years to achieve a settlement and, even though interim payments may be given, the sufferers sometimes die before settlement is reached. The bronchitis/emphysema cases compose the largest single piece of litigation known in this country and possibly in the world."

Bronchitis and emphysema are also described as chronic obstructive airways disease. The symptoms include coughing and breathlessness, even after minor exertion. It can be caused by smoking but those exposed to dust can develop it more readily than the ordinary population. It can also take the form of pneumoconiosis which can be severe and result in rapid deterioration.

"Vibration white finger. There are 19,000 cases pending but a case can take

up to fifteen months to settle. Employers are not liable before 1975 when the cause of this condition was finally established."
(Hand – arm syndrome, also known as vibration white finger, causes pain and numbness in the parts of the body which are repeatedly exposed to intense vibration from machinery. It develops slowly and intermittently. Fingers become pale or blue and sufferers have difficulty in manipulating small objects or in dressing themselves.
Fifteen months to settle refers to the period of time between the case being accepted by the Union, through various medical procedures, to the final hearing before a tribunal or court).
"Deafness. This was acknowledged as an industrial illness in 1963 and usually takes 6 or 7 months to settle. There are 4,000 cases awaiting agreement."
"Asthma. This can be made worse by industrial conditions but can be difficult to prove.

Many of the above cases are in Nottinghamshire. (The situation is made worse by the fact that many miners' records were destroyed when mines were closed, especially in the 1980s and 1990s.)
However, when claims do reach court they are between 70 and 80% successful."

The Evening Post Campaign
The 'Post' has fought vigorously for justice for disabled miners. Here an article comments on the compensation system.
"In a string of hard-hitting exclusives the 'Post' has highlighted the frustrating obstacles faced by sick former miners making cash claims. In December 1999, we were told by the Government it would take two years to settle all the claims from men suffering from chronic bronchitis and emphysema. Twelve months later, this had risen to FIVE years. (This is still an under estimate – see above)."
The article goes on to describe the procedures and tests involved and concludes:
"This lengthy process has opened the system up to accusations of red tape.
'It is still appalling,' said UDM general secretary Mick Stevens. 'We are having miners dying while waiting for claims.'"
Things have moved on, for in March 2001 the 'Post' reported how one sufferer had at last received compensation:
"Yet Mr. Kettleworth (not his real name) believes that the five-figure pay out is too little too late. He took voluntary redundancy from Cotgrave Colliery in 1993 .... and then he could play cricket and football .... Now his lungs have become so badly damaged by the choking coal dust that he is 90% disabled."
In the case of vibration white finger, the paper announced in May 1999:
"NOTTS ex-miners with crippled hands were today set to pass £2m landmark in their seven-year compensation battle .... The government announced a

£500m compensation package on January 22 .... The settlement was followed in March by a £1bn deal for ex-miners with chest diseases.
Sherwood MP Paddy Tipping commented 'These men worked hard all their lives for our benefit. I am chuffed this money is finally getting through.'"

Nurses at the Pit
'I know now why they call you Flatty Bates.'
Medical provision at the pits was improving and it became usual to have a fully trained nurse on duty. Norman cannot praise them enough, but he always wondered why one was nicknamed 'Flatty Bates'. It was certainly not her physique. One day he found out:

"One day I dropped a big block of wood on me thumb and clacked me nail. And this nail was giving me gyp. All the colours, purple, black and everything. But it was throbbing like nobody's business. Come up the pit and sat in the canteen with this still throbbing and somebody said, 'Go and see Flatty Bates. She'll sort you out.' So I went straight down the medical centre. 'What's the matter Norman?' - because the sisters at the pit all knew your name. 'I've blacked me thumbnail.' She says 'Alright, I'll sort you out. Put your arm on the chair.'

She grabbed hold of my wrist with one hand. You couldn't shift it. It was like having a G clamp on your hand. And I started wondering what's she going to do. There were beads of perspiration on my forehead. Then with her other hand she went into this tray and came out with a flat needle which she then shoved right down me nail and gave it a wiggle about either side. Me shouting and screaming, trying to be brave. But the relief of the pain was such that I came out of there and stopped at the door and I turned round to her and I said I know now why they call you Flatty Bates and she gave me a smile and a wink and says 'Watch your fingers in future.' And she was renowned for black fingernails and boils.'

"There were beads of perspiration on my forehead."

PART SIX: The fifties and sixties

'A very lively mining community.'

Galas

Miners still accounted for a large part of Nottinghamshire life. A brief glance at the 1950s editions of weekly newspaper, 'The Hucknall Dispatch' gives an impression of a very lively mining community. Hardly a week went by without some mention of miners' galas, brass band concerts, the selection of a coal queen and trips for retired miners and their wives. As well as the occasional headline featuring a miner being accused of some drunken foolishness on a Friday night.

The NCB magazine 'Coal' paints a similar picture and the edition for October 1950 has reports from all over the country. The following is a news item about Gedling:

'Veterans Join Pensioners' Outing. Ninety five retired employees at Gedling Colliery, Nottingham, attended the annual outing of the Old Age Pensioners. With them were 25 men over 65 years of age still at work, all of whom have completed more than 50 years in the industry. Oldest member of the party was Mr. J. Wells, Daybrook, 83; with the longest service, Mr. F. Lang, Arnold, 78, with 64 years' service; and the oldest member still working, Mr Beedall, Mapperley, 72.'

There was all the fun of the fair at the first East Midlands Gala at Alfreton and the first Nottinghamshire 'demonstration' at Cinderhill.

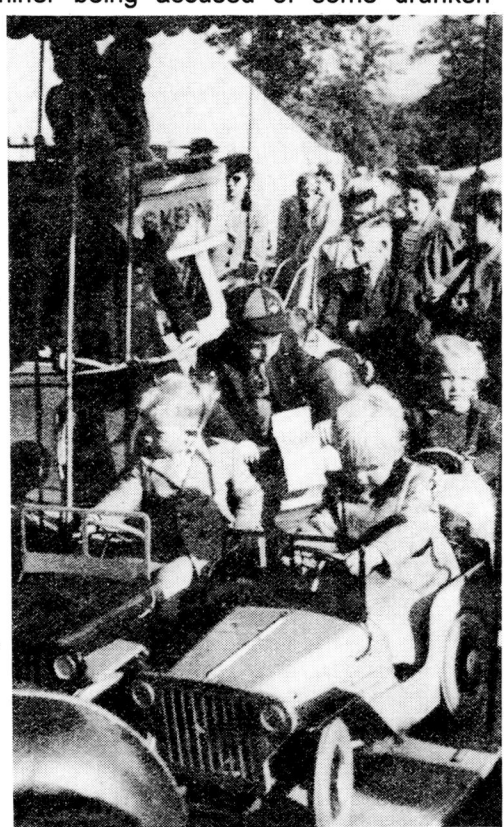

Roundabout and sideshows at the East Midlands Gala in 1950 (photo: 'Coal' magazine)

Nottinghamshire Miners' Tales

Subsidence
'Hucknall is an area suffering greatly from an industry nationally owned'
There are also frequent reports of local concerns about subsidence. The edition for September 25th 1952 provides an interesting example and quotes comments made during a meeting of Hucknall Urban Council;
'HUCKNALL HOUSES SINKING. One third of Hucknall is badly affected by mining subsidence.... Reports during the month showed a settlement of up to 4½ inches beneath post war council houses at Johnson Avenue and considerable subsidence in the west of the town.
Hucknall is an area suffering greatly from an industry nationally owned and the community should be compensated.'
Month after month the council minutes express concern about further instances of subsidence.
The *Nottingham Evening Post* for the summer of 1955 has articles about the coal strike in Yorkshire as well as warnings about productivity and the possibility of encouraging miners from abroad to come and work in British pits. There was also news of a ten shilling rise per ton in the cost of domestic coal.

The Honeymoon is Over
There was also growing disillusionment with the effects of nationalisation. Councillor Riddell:
"There was tension between the managers who were engineers by training, and the other managers who tended to be professional people from outside the industry or from the NUM.... The engineers under private enterprise had made the decisions."
For a time the unions became part of management but the character of the Coal Board changed under the 1951 Conservative Government and *"The mining engineers and colliery management fought a rearguard action very successfully.... People like myself felt that the Coal Board was not a place where one could work and do a constructive job because once more it was the engineers, the colliery managers who were in control."*
During the 1950s, well over 100 pits in the country were closed but there was little opposition because there were plenty of jobs elsewhere. Six Nottinghamshire collieries closed, to be followed in the 1960s by a further nine including Clifton, Kirkby, Langton, Selston and Brookhill, all of which closed in 1968.
But the South Notts coalfield was the most productive in Britain and it was coal from more recently opened pits such as Calverton in 1952 and Cotgrave in 1964 which supplied the newly developed power stations in the Trent Valley. There was also Bevercotes in the north of the county, described as the 'world's first fully automated pit.' New records in production were set. For example in 1966, Summit Pit in Kirkby hoisted the Union Jack when over one million tons were produced, but by 1969 the pit was closed which *'came as a bolt from the blue'* and had a devastating effect on the community.

Competition from Oil and Gas
Coal was facing increasing competition from oil and natural gas so that by the end of the sixties it had become commonplace, even in Nottinghamshire, for new houses to be built without a traditional fireplace. Instead there was central heating and a gas or electric fire in the living room. There was also growing concern about the effect on the atmosphere of the burning of fossil fuels, including the damage caused by acid rain to buildings, forests and lakes. Smokeless fuel was introduced, which was more expensive and, in the opinion of many, less efficient than ordinary coal. Non-mining folk living near a mining community remember:
"We had to burn the smokeless fuel but the miners still used their free coal and thick black smoke came out of their chimneys."

Sharing the Good Times and the Bad
'But it was a happy pit.'

In spite of all the problems associated with working underground many miners say, *"But it was a happy pit."* Norman Beadle:
"It was the 'crack' (banter). The one liners. I remember I broke my foot and they had to put me on a pony to get me to the pit bottom. Every jolt was agony and when I came out of the roads on the pony the others were waiting to go back on top. As soon as he saw me, one of them said, 'Look lads 'ere comes Jesus.' "

But news of an accident had a profound effect on morale.
Norman:
"I was sat in the Welfare one night and someone came in and says so and so has been killed down pit. The word went round like wildfire…. Everybody was absolutely stunned into silence. You know it can't happen. It don't happen at our pit. We hadn't had fatalities. Everyone looked after one another. For a couple or three weeks everybody were on a lull so to speak… There wasn't the happiness they were all grieving, even people who didn't know him well."

Pithead Baths
'It'll be alright lads. It'll come off on the sheets.'

By the 1950s, showers were in place throughout the mining industry. The first had been installed in the 1930s, but had been received with caution by older miners, partly through embarrassment, but also fear of catching their *'death of cold'* or, more seriously, of picking up skin infections.
In 1976, Carl Chamberlain, who was then 19, recalls his first visit to North Colliery, Hucknall:
"…. when I first got there you entered the pit baths and it was red hot and there were naked men running about in the showers and I was a bit young and I was a bit amazed by this. And all spraying cold water in the showers messing about."

However some miners were still not too particular.
Norman explains:
"Bacca Baines had been a miner I think since he were about three years of age because what Bacca didn't know about pit were nobody's business, And nobody could beat Bacca Baines into the Welfare. He used to come up out of the pit and as he was coming out of the lamp cabin after he'd put his lamp back on charge, his clothes started coming off. His coat and his vest went into his helmet and by the time he got into the baths all he'd got to take off was his trousers, his pit boots and his socks. And he just used to bung them in the locker and get his towel and his soap and into the showers. He'd lather up his head and with the soap bubbles what was running down his body he used to wash all over. The one thing he never washed was his back. You could see a line where he used to have a permanent square on his back. We used to shout at him, 'Bacca, I'll give your back a wash.' 'It'll be alright lads, it'll come off on sheets. Our Aggie will see to that."

Snuff
Norman continues:
'Bacca Baines used to take a tin of snuff a day, a big tin of McChrystal snuff a day. A lot of miners took snuff and they still do. I think old Bacca he were addicted to snuff because he would take it in the Welfare and he'd have a handkerchief which was permanently stained brown …. How Agnes put up with him with bed sheets and his handkerchiefs I shall never know to this day.'
Miners usually took snuff because they could not smoke underground and the floor of the mine would be littered with the empty tins. Flavoured chewing tobacco was also a favourite.
Stan Stanton started at Cotgrave in 1972:
"You had to be with somebody for about a month to find your way round, make sure you weren't doing anything you shouldn't do and carrying anything you shouldn't carry…..Obviously you weren't allowed to carry cigarettes down the pit which was quite easy to do because people would light a cigarette before they went down the mine. Well it was quite easy to put them in your overall pocket and walk down, so they used to have people searching you. Three people random stopping people and they would just search you and if they found cigarettes on you well you'd be down the road looking for a job…..I used to take a lot of snuff. And tobacco, I tried it , where they used to chew tobacco, but it wasn't something I enjoyed. But McChrystal snuff, yes, you could have white snuff, brown snuff, strawberry snuff. It was every sort of snuff.'

The Hoax Calls
By 1961 mining employment in Nottinghamshire reached its peak of 56,000 but gradually miners' wages had slipped below the average for other heavy industries. Still, by the 1970s the mood in the mining industry was

changing, which perhaps explains the hoax calls to the Mines Rescue Service. One of the last was from Clifton but the Ilkeston team arrived at the colliery first and made radio contact so that the Mansfield vehicle was able to turn back. Three separate calls at intervals were made from Rufford stating that a bomb had been planted. On the first two occasions the afternoon shift was cleared from the mine but by the third time the miners simply refused to evacuate the pit with the rejoinder, *"Well you come down here and find the bomb."*

George Burton, now retired, but an officer at Mansfield Rescue Station during the 1960s, describes what happened at Bentinck:

"Another one was Bentinck. I was third officer then. It had took us three weeks to put these massive seals on 2 intake and I return (this was to prevent a large heating becoming a full blown fire) and we had completed and finished. Three or four days later I conducted an underground training with one of the Bentinck Colliery teams. We had done firefighting and we also examined one of the stoppings. We left the pit and returned to the station and when everything was checked I used to go and have my shower and it would have been about 3 o'clock and the alarm bell went. Everybody was running to the turnout vehicle, me included, with towel around me and soaped all over. I got on the vehicle and I changed quickest because my pit clothes were in my hand."

George Burton

Once at the pit, George and the superintendent reported to the management who sent deputies and overmen to check the stoppings. They returned to say, *"We haven't had an explosion."*

"The report was there had been an explosion at one of the stoppings. Another hoax call. And the man had given the name of the safety officer. He'd given the name of the district, given the name of the stopping. Everything. Knew everything.

(By now it was 4 o'clock and the team were anxious to leave.) *They sat on the vehicle saying 'Come on George. Come on.' So I went and checked the rescue room because there was always the possibility they'd left equipment behind. Then I ran straight to the van and these contract labourers were resurfacing that deep* (indicates) *in concrete the new pit top and there were these two men with vibrating or levelling motors on the end of a plank (to smooth off the cement). I got halfway and suddenly realised I'm up to my ankles in concrete. So I stopped and they said, 'You might as well continue.' But the hoax calls stopped because we changed our procedure and spoke to someone in authority at the pit by VHF radio whilst responding to the call."*

Nottinghamshire Miners' Tales 55

Underwater Training

However, the rescue service continued its work of training teams to react to problems underground. Disasters often resulted in new procedures being introduced. This was the case after the Lofthouse disaster in Yorkshire, 21st March, 1973.

The official report states:

'The inrush was sudden and violent and water flowed in both directions along the face.'

Seven men lost their lives, but only one body was recovered.

It was felt that in future all members of the rescue service should be able to function in diving gear. The training was done in a swimming pool and the aim was for the team to be able to pick their way through obstacles in pitch black conditions underwater and underground. They did not want men who could swim, because rescuers would have to find their way along the roads around submerged rubble and machinery. It was difficult at first because the team, although wearing breathing apparatus, instinctively stopped breathing once they were under water.

George explains:

"The biggest thing was breathe. I said to them you've got apparatus on. You've been breathing up there why aren't you breathing now? When you go under water it's your instinct to hold your breath. But you must breathe. The next thing was to walk along the side. Then when they started to go further out we had to have weights made because otherwise the inflation of the breathing apparatus would lift you off the ground. Next they had to walk a width underwater. They had got a rope around their waist and a tennis ball in their hand so that they could let it go if they were in difficulties. Later, we put obstacles under the water, mainly tubular chairs all over the place. Finally they had to do it all wearing blacked out goggles."

The Medical

'I ran down the pub last night and it nearly killed me.'

It is not surprising that a high level of fitness and courage was needed by all men in the rescue teams at the pit and in the service.

Stan was a member of the rescue team at Cotgrave:

"You had to take a medical every year which was exactly the same as the Forces medical. It's a very very good medical. So you had to keep yourself pretty fit. You had to do so many trainings a year at different collieries, the Mines Rescue Station at Mansfield and Ashby. There was the Pack Test. They used to put you on a treadmill machine for 7 minutes, walking at a very brisk pace and then it used to go into an incline…. They'd put you on a heart machine before you started and then as soon as you came off the machine. They'd lie you down for so many minutes to see how quick your heart recovery rate is and you used to have a back pack on. I can't remember what it was. A third of your body weight or something like that. And then obviously

Cotgrave Rescue Team wearing green helmets to identify them during rescue work. Stan Stanton is second from right

your heartbeat had to get back to a certain level….When I knew my medical was coming up I would stop drinking and make sure I trained…. I could remember one guy, Mick, he was a bit of a character to say the least. He was about 6ft 2 or 6ft 3. Always very fit but he never done any sports. He was just a naturally fit bloke. When we used to go for a medical people used to say, 'Have you done any training then Mick?' and he'd say 'Oh yes I ran down the pub last night and it nearly killed me.' And he was always one of the fittest.

My heartbeat never changed for nine years on the trot. The doctor used to say he was amazed because you're getting older and your heart should take longer to recover."

There was also a urine test. On one occasion Norman was helping the nurse by doing the test on the specimens. He came up with an unusual result.

"I showed it to the nurse and she said, 'That does happen sometimes but I'll have to have a word with him. Go and fetch him.' I came back with a very fit looking young miner. The nurse said ,'Excuse me but I have to ask you this. Did you have sexual intercourse last night?' He beamed at her and he said, 'Yes. And I had it again this morning."

Nottinghamshire Miners' Tales   57

Sports Days

All miners had to be strong in order to do their job and many were keen sportsmen.

Stan:

"…. There was a lot of sport at Cotgrave. Always had a football team. I used to play for the cricket team at Cotgrave. They had their own snooker team. Sports day at Cotgrave used to be a great day and I can say they played a pretty good standard at most of the sports…. Some kept whippets and then there were the pigeon men. I think a lot of that originated from Durham. When I was about 19 years of age, Cotgrave was full of Geordie people – very funny people, good hard workers."

The Welfare
'A fantastic place. You'd get two thousand people in there on Fridays and Saturdays.'

Carl:

"At Hucknall The Welfare was absolutely brilliant. A fantastic place. You'd get 2,000 people in there on Fridays and Saturdays, upstairs and downstairs. Massive Stage, they used to have some proper big bands on. They've had bands there when they've been number 1 in the charts in the 70's because they'd got the money. They could pay the money. We had Slade there, had some top class entertainers. That was the centre of Hucknall. They used to come from miles around to the Welfare…. You could be an associate member if you wasn't a miner ….They used to put on art exhibitions, miners' work….It was the place to go and meet…. It's been knocked down."

Miners were generous in contributing to local charities. Cotgrave miners raised funds for a children's ward at The Queens Medical Centre and Carl

Cotgrave team taking part in the Skegness to Nottingham charity walk

remembers how, in common with other collieries, Hucknall miners agreed to having a regular sum taken out of their pay. There was also the annual Skegness to Nottingham Walk in which Stan and a team from Cotgrave took part and raised over £2,000 for the children's ward. Local charities were badly affected when the mines closed.

PART SEVEN: The Turbulent Years

The Job Interview 1970s Style
'In 1976 me uncle who worked on the surface was retiring so me Dad took me down to fill his place.'

By the late 1970s, miners wore orange work wear which, together with personal safety equipment including helmets, became standard issue. But even though time had moved on there were some things which remained very similar. Take, for instance, Stan's job interview at Cotgrave in 1972:

"I'd never been down a pit in my life and I decided I had to get out of Wales really so I arranged to come up to my sister's for a weekend and I went for an interview on the Monday morning and as soon as I said my brother-in-law worked there it was 'Oh right. Start next Monday on your training."

Carl was 19 in 1976 and:
"In 1976 me uncle who worked on the surface was retiring so me Dad took me down to fill his place. So it was another Chamberlain at North Colliery."

Geoff Blore joined Newstead pit in 1976 after several years in the army:
"There were always jobs in mining then because of the high turnover. I had a medical. They checked my eyesight and hearing and I had a general physical. We were issued with two brass checks. You handed one in at the pit top and kept the other in your pocket.... The mine was infested with mice. A friend of mine nearly died because he accidentally put his hand on one and it bit him. Mice carry hepatitus.

By now the ponies had left the pit and young trainees followed a proper course to prepare them for work underground; for many this was at Bentinck Colliery near Kirkby or, as in Stan and Carl's case, Moorgreen. So some things were the same, but much had changed beyond recognition, as Geoff describes:

"I lived in Newstead Colliery village for about two years, but then I commuted from Nottingham. There was a bus service but lots of miners had a car or a

Nottinghamshire Miners' Tales

motorbike and there was a large car park at the pit."
However, Carl explains:

"I lived half a mile from the pit…. Most lived in walking distance really or bike."

Working on the Pit Top at Hucknall
During the years he was at Hucknall, Carl always worked on the pit top:
"We were loading materials for the face and whatever, the arches and all the timber chock blocks. We had a sawmill where we sawed the split bars for shoring the roof. All mining equipment we used to strip down and send it underground. It was a bit arduous all through the winter. I could remember at one stage we were working where the air intake is and it was minus 25, somebody brought in a thermometer. So they issued us with thermal underwear, balaclava helmet and thick moleskin trousers and jackets. My wife Mandy said I looked like a big teddy bear covered in frost."

The men working on the pit top were a team of skilled tradesmen as well as labourers. There were blacksmiths, joiners and bricklayers as well as specially trained crane drivers. There was also great variety in the job.
Carl:
"If there was a spillage down the line I used to enjoy that. We used to go right down towards the lakes at Bestwood Country Park. Sometimes the coal wagons used to go round the corner there and spill the coal onto the track so the railway had to be cleared. ….we used to take a shovel and used to walk the track. Like being in an American film. You just walked the lines down the track and just cleared the coal off the lines. Take all day out in the country. A good shift that.'

Working Underground at Cotgrave
'It gets faster and faster as you're going down hill …. And you say to yourself 'Do I stay or do I jump?'

Stan worked underground at Cotgrave and says that many miners were trained for other jobs:
"There was a guy driving the trains with us who was a qualified schoolteacher, got qualified bricklayers, carpenters, every sort of person you could think. And we used to say, 'Well surely if you're a schoolteacher you'd be better off not doing this.' But he said, 'Yes but I can earn more than I could teaching."

Underground, Cotgrave pit stretched for many miles - in one direction as far as Holme Pierrepont - and under a number of villages, though mining beneath a church was forbidden. So it covered a big area and conditions varied between the different seams, some areas being dry and dusty and others, like the Black Shale being wet.
Stan:
"We always seemed to have problems with the Black Shale coal. Every time you went down there the floor comes up very quick, the roof comes in very

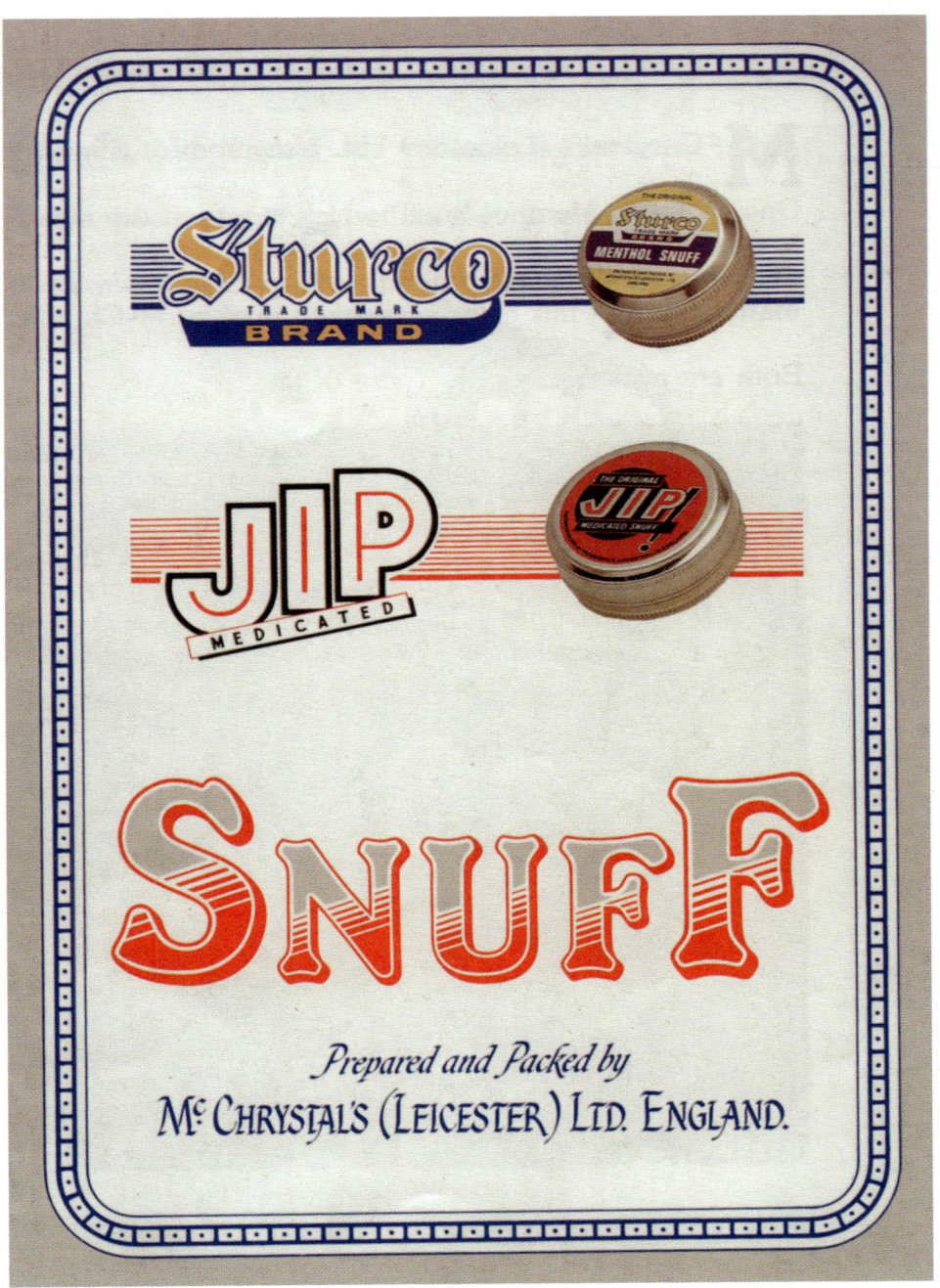

With cigarettes banned, snuff was popular with miners working underground. McChrystal's were major manufacturers of the product

Nottinghamshire Miners' Tales

quick. So like you could be a mile in and the floor behind you is coming up all the time so you were what you call dinting it all the time."

Sometimes the seams were quite low but when Stan left Cotgrave they had seams which were up to 10ft wide and *'You could walk through it like walking through your house.'* The job which Stan enjoyed most was driving the train but it was dangerous if you ignored the rules:

"You were only supposed to pull five full wagons a shift because there was the limit on the weight you were supposed to pull with the train. And then you were only allowed to bring so many empties plus full ones back out with you. Plus you've got to think underground it's not flat and you've got gradients uphill, downhill and if you get a train on what you call a runaway it's very dangerous. You've got too much weight behind the train so when you apply your brakes they lock onto the track and then it's just steel to steel and the train runs away. And of course it gets faster and faster because you are going downhill. You say to yourself, 'Do I stay with it or do I jump out?' And we've had quite a few people jump out and let the train go. And you just see a big puff of smoke and a big bang and it's all off the track sideways up in the air....

"I can remember a certain guy (who had a runaway) 'phoned me and my mate Bobber....because if they had an accident with the train we had to take all the equipment out to get the train back on the rails, take lifting gear all that

Battery-powered engine at Cotgrave for manriding and handling supplies

sort of thing. We got there and he had something like four times as many wagons on as he should have had on and we knew the inspectors would come in so we had to like move the wagons quick."

But sometimes taking risks could lead to a tragic loss of life.

Stan:

"There was a good friend of mine, Steve, and he actually got killed when he was doing his face training at Cotgrave…..And they'd been working on night shift, as the story goes. The men had all come along the face to come out because they'd walked the main gateway because of the better air. But they'd been working the tailgate side and Steve had left his flask at the other end and he decided to go back for it and he's thinking he's going to be late getting out of the pit. He jumped on the coal conveyor which it is totally illegal to do – this is how the story came out – and he went to get off and got stuck and went under the machine and them machines don't give you two chances."

The 1970s Strike and Go Slow

By 1970, of the 958 mines that had been nationalised in 1947, just three hundred remained, and even though the NUM had a moderate leader in Joe Gormley, the general trend was to the left. It was to be a confusing decade.

On the one hand, by 1974, instead of providing one half of Britain's energy needs as it had in the sixties, coal was contributing just one third. But a huge rise in oil prices made coal competitive again, although this reprieve was to

Coal-picking at Kirkby in 1972 (Nottingham Evening Post)

Clipstone Colliery headstocks

be a temporary one. It was also the decade in which miners supported the first national strike since 1926. This lasted seven weeks at the end of which miners were awarded most of what they had demanded, though not before coal picking at Kirkby and a soup kitchen at Cotgrave had returned as a grim reminder of the 1920s.

Soup kitchen at Cotgrave in 1974 (Nottingham Evening Post)

'Well, lads, how long is this going to last then?'

The troubles were far from over. Late in 1973, the NUM called an overtime ban which lasted into the following year and had a devastating effect on the economy and the government. It is remembered as a time of national emergency when industry was on a three-day week, there were regular power cuts, and restrictions were set on heating and lighting in public places. This affected everyone. There were, for instance, no evening classes and younger people became aware of what the City Centre must have been like during the wartime blackout, for only essential street lighting was allowed and shop windows were in darkness.

Barry Heath, now retired, but then on picket duty at Clipstone, recalls it vividly but says the idea that relations between the police and the miners were all bad is quite wrong:

"I was on picket duty and we had a brazier to keep us warm. The police sergeant came over to join us. 'Well lads' he said, 'how long is this going to last then?' 'Till they meet our demands .' 'Oh good. I could do with a bit of overtime.'"

Those on picket duty, especially at night time, also kept a sense of proportion:

"We had a rota for going down the pub. One chap was so late getting back that the rest of us had to leave him on his own so that we could get a pint in before closing time. It was all good humoured and he tried to make out he was afraid of the dark."

An Incident at Stavely
'I was still struggling into my clothes when I went out into the bitter cold.'

The Rescue Service never went on strike, and Norman Beadle remembers an incident at Ireland Pit near Stavely:

"The bells went off at four in the morning and I jumped into my britches which were always left at side of the bed. Jean went down to open the front door and lock it behind me. I was still struggling into my clothes when I went out into the bitter cold. There must have been twelve inches of fine powdery snow. We'd been called to the Ireland pit at Stavely. A plume of smoke was emerging from the upcast shaft near the fan Evarsay. But first of all we had to convince the pickets to let us in. They thought it was a trick of the management. We did all the checks but it was the engineer who had turned up, who suddenly realised the smoke was the hot air condensing as it came out of the upcast shaft into the intense cold. By now the deputies had arrived and also the police. There was some trouble. Some vandalism but it fizzled out. We went and reported to the manager and asked him if we could have some coal because we were all short of coal. We loaded so much into the number one Emergency Van that it could hardly move. I went in the smaller van with someone else and we managed to 'rescue' some railway sleepers which was lying about. We covered them with our jackets and suddenly the manager of the Mines Rescue tapped on the window and asked us for a lift to his car on the other side of the yard. The three of us sat in the front. He glanced in the back but he didn't seem to notice nothing and we thought we'd got away with it but as he was getting out he said, 'When you've chopped that lot up you can put my share in the boot of my car."

In 1974 Edward Heath called a General Election, seen as a trial of strength with the unions, and lost. A Labour Government came to power and was in office until 1979 during which time a further 32 pits closed. However, the miners had won the first battle and could, it appeared, only go from strength to strength. By 1984, the Conservatives, under the leadership of Margaret Thatcher, had a 100 seat majority and Arthur Scargill, a leftwinger, was the leader of the NUM.

Severe cutbacks in the iron and steel industry in the early 1980s meant that coal was losing its biggest customer. In 1981, thirty pits, which even the NCB acknowledged would have to close, were saved by a government concession, thus averting a strike. It is said that the government only saved these pits because they were not yet fully prepared for the coal strike which they knew was inevitable. Coal stocks were being built up at the power stations.

> *"When you've chopped that lot up you can put my share in the boot of my car."*

PART EIGHT: The 1984/85 strike

The Struggle Begins.
'It were miner against miner.'

On March 1st 1984, it was announced that Cortonwood Colliery in Yorkshire was to close. By Monday March 12th a strike was in progress and during those first days, a young Yorkshire miner, 24-year old David Gareth Jones, collapsed and died shortly after leaving the picket line at Ollerton because he had sustained crush injuries. This tragic event was the grim foreshadowing of the bitter and violent struggle which was to follow.

The Contenders Comment
In her autobiography, 'The Downing Street Years' Margaret Thatcher devotes a chapter to the strike entitled *'Mr Scargill's Insurrection.'* In her opinion:
'.... *The NUM and the fear it inspired came into the hands of those whose objectives were openly political.'*
Arthur Scargill stated his agenda in *'The Morning Star'* of March 28th when he wrote:
'....*the NUM is engaged in a social and industrial Battle of Britain.... What is urgently needed is the rapid and total mobilisation of the Trade Union and Labour Movement.'*

Violence Erupts
'The Miners' Dispute. A Catalogue of Violence,' published by the National Working Miners' Committee states:
'From the first day of this dispute until 7a.m. Wednesday 3rd October, 7121 persons have been arrested for offences in connection with the dispute, 790 police officers have been injured of whom 65 suffered serious injuries, 2 miners have committed suicide, 2 have died as a result of picket line violence

The Miners' Dispute over Pit Closures 1983 · 84 · 85

A postcard published by J/V Postcards (Arthur Veasey and Paul Judson) in 1984 featuring the chief protagonists in the strike, Arthur Scargill and Ian MacGregor

and 255 miners have been reported injured.'
And the strike, which did not end until February 1985, still had over four months to run.
Entry in *'The Catalogue'* for March 15th:
'Violence occurred at Ollerton Colliery near Mansfield, where 7 police officers were hurt trying to prevent three hundred pickets from blockading the main gate as the 450 man day shift arrived for work.
Five pickets were arrested, working miners were punched, and police were pelted with bricks, lumps of wood, milk bottles and fireworks.'

The Striking Miners

But the miners, whatever their politics, found themselves caught up in a fight to save jobs. In 1984, Arthur Scargill forecast that 70 pits would close at a cost of 70,000 jobs. It was an underestimate for, by 1990, 101 had been closed. Geoff Blore recalls his own reaction at Newstead in 1984:
"I thought that the miners who were against the strike were short-sighted and had been got at by the Conservatives. I didn't like Scargill. He was too abrasive but I sensed the truth of what he was saying. He could have done with an image make over like they gave Thatcher. She was determined to break the unions. It was like the ancient struggle between Rome and Carthage. Thatcher was Rome - and it was a case of 'Cartago delenda est' (Carthage must go)."

Geoff joined the picket lines at his own colliery:
"There was definitely media manipulation. I remember on one occasion I had been picketing at Newstead and, without provocation, the police charged us so we retaliated by throwing stuff at them. But on the News that evening it was made to look as if we had started the trouble."

The Police

The police came in for a lot of criticism, especially from the Left, because they had the power to stop striking miners from entering the county in excessive numbers to join picket lines, and the cars of intending pickets were frequently stopped and turned back between Nottingham and Doncaster. From the police perspective, their role was to uphold the democratic rights of miners so that, free from intimidation, those who wanted to work and those who wanted to take part in peaceful picketing, could do so. They also patrolled the colliery villages to protect local families from harassment.

Part of the huge police presence in Nottinghamshire during the 1984 strike (photo: John Harris. National Museum of Labour History)

An incident from *The Catalogue:*
'SEPTEMBER 22nd
'Mr. Albert Taylor of Mansfield Woodhouse .... stopped going to work for a period after finding three men outside his house who told him: 'We will not

Nottinghamshire Miners' Tales

stop you going to work but bear in mind you have got a wife and three kids in there.' He had frequently received threatening calls throughout the night and the word 'Scab' had been daubed on his car.'
This type of incident was unusual, but working miners were grateful for police protection, though some people came to perceive the police as "*Mrs Thatcher's henchmen.*"
In their introduction, Jim Coulter, Susan Miller and Martin Walker who wrote 'Miners' Strike 1984. Politics and Policing in the Coal Fields.' state:
'.... The miners and their families are talking about the survival of their class and their community.... The miners' strike has come about because of brutal economic policies.'

A chapter is devoted to:
'The Dirty War in Nottingham.... Torture in Rainworth.... Kidnap in Blidworth.' in which striking miners from outside the county who were staying in the pit villages accuse the police of brutal treatment.
However, the Nottinghamshire Constabulary has always had good relations with the mining community for 'if you scratch a local bobby you will find a direct line to the mining industry.' Ex-miners have joined the local police force for years and continued to do so after the strike. It was usually policemen who were drafted in from outside who over-reacted, though they would strongly deny accusations of brutality.

Carl Chamberlain:
"We were going down to work in the morning and you'd get people like being assaulted and things, just unbelievable you know. And cars were damaged and things, just crazy things 'cos it were miner against miner. You'd see Metropolitan Police which you knew were London police by the white shirt.... only the Met had the white shirt and tie with the Met. Badge on. You'd see gangs of these roaming around and I thought what's happening? Why have these been drafted in? They took a harder line than our police because our police had said to the unions 'We've got to live with these people....when it's all over.' So the London Met were brought in.'

The Nottinghamshire Women's Support Group
'I'll never eat bloody beans on toast after the strike.'
The miners in Nottinghamshire who supported the stoppage were always in the minority. At first 10,000 came out on strike in the county, but this figure dwindled to 2,500 as the strike progressed. These men and their families became increasingly bitter because, in their view, they were making enormous sacrifices to save the jobs of all miners. Joan Witham's book, 'Hearts and Minds,' describes the work of the Nottinghamshire Women's Support Group, which extended right across the county and was composed of the wives of striking miners. They had a great deal of support in Britain and from abroad, with help coming from Russia. Even Colonel Gaddafi in Libya gave encouragement. The women set up soup kitchens and learned to enjoy

Rally of striking miners in Nottingham's Market Square in April 1984 (National Museum of Labour History)

the strange foreign food which arrived:

A miner's wife from Linby:

"We had some fun when foreign food came. Nobody could read the labels, we had to go by what was in the picture, if there was one.... Someone said they fed some to their dog and it nearly died, but I think that was a joke."

But much of the food that arrived consisted of stodge, especially tins of baked beans, and one heartfelt cry was:

"I'll never eat bloody beans on toast after the strike, they're coming out of my bloody ears.'"

The group set up a stall in Nottingham City Centre and met with both support and abuse but:

"It gave the collectors pleasure to fix a 'Coal not Dole' sticker to a Jaeger suit."

Some of the women spoke to a wide variety of groups; even going as far afield as America, where they found that some of their supporters lived and worked under far worse conditions than they did. They often felt intimidated and roughly treated by the police, but they believed that at long last they had grown up and it was a personal triumph:

Support from Hertfordshire: banner of St Albans Group (National Museum of Labour History)

"We lived on £20 a week for 5 adults, but we never went hungry because we had so much help…. I had never even met a black person, now we stay with them in London and they are my friends."'

But as time went on, things became more difficult and their numbers decreased:

"It wasn't funny having sacks of potatoes in your front room either, especially when they started to smell. You couldn't move the damned things."

It was just before Christmas that things got really bad:

"But the worst was the cold…. We burnt furniture…. We burnt shoes. We chopped up our wooden ladder."

While the women felt that "*horizons were extended and bonds formed*" their children and husbands did not always understand or agree. But it was not only the women who were aware of support for the striking miners.

Geoff Blore:

"My son collected on the streets of London. He stayed with a family down there in St Albans and is still in touch with them."

NUM pickets keep warm outside Bevercotes Colliery near Mansfield in March 1984 (National Museum of Labour History)

"It wasn't funny having sacks of potatoes in your front room."

Nottinghamshire Miners' Tales

The Right to a Ballot
'If Scargill had gone round it the right way in the beginning he would have got every miner in the country to come out on strike.'
The miners who continued to work felt they too were fighting for an important principle.
Stan:
"If Scargill had gone round it the right way in the beginning he would have got every miner in the country to come out on strike. But because he was dictating to the miners that they would go on strike, without a democratic vote basically, I think he got a lot of the Nottinghamshire miners' backs up as well as a lot of the other miners. And as we said at the end of the day we're entitled to a vote and he was trying to put miners on strike without voting.'

They were not impressed by Ian MacGregor and the NCB either. Many of those involved in the dispute came to bitterly regret the loss of dignity and respect suffered by the whole of the mining industry.

Right to work rally outside the NUM headquarters at Mansfield in May 1984(National Museum of Labour History)

The Pickets
Stan Stanton remembers going through the pickets at Cotgrave:
"Thousands of them. I actually drove along from Cotgrave one day and I've never seen so many pickets in my life and I mean thousands and thousands. They were kicking cars and everything and in the end we heard there was a load of Yorkshire pickets coming down and we decided to leave the cars at home and go in on the bus. And they were throwing things at the bus and shouting, 'Scabs.' And there were even people at our own pit that had gone on strike…. If you were on afternoon shift, if they'd been in the pub as well before, they'd just get rowdier and rowdier, and there was one old guy come through the picket lines at Cotgrave and they literally smashed his car to bits. His windscreen, the lot, and this bloke was like nearly 60 and he never worked again… the police actually escorted him home, but he never come back to work again.'.

Working miners also wondered how the pickets could afford to drink in pubs and travel to different pits.

The UDM
After the strike finished, in February 1985, the old working relationships did not return.
Stan:
"The problem was that Cotgrave had UDM and NUM people working side by side and some people never spoke to their friends ever again. It was the same with fathers and sons. We had a particular family, the son was a big UDM man and the father was an NUM and I don't think they ever spoke again. A lot of them never came back. Some of them got transferred to North Notts pits where a lot of them were NUM pits. Yes, there was a lot went to Harworth…. I went on to Stoke on a mechanical course for a week and there was two guys on the same course from a pit up North somewhere and they were NUM and as soon as they found out we were from Nottingham they turned round to the guy on the course and said, 'We're not coming tomorrow.' And they dropped out of the course…. I think the strike was the death of the pits because once the unions split you got no muscle at all."

By July 1985 the miners of Nottingham, under the leadership of Neil Greatrex, Roy Lynk and Dave Prendergast, had voted to cede from the NUM. The UDM (Union of Democratic Mineworkers) was in existence by the end of the year and was initially very successful, with a membership of 37,000.

> *"Some people never spoke to their friends again."*

Nottinghamshire Miners' Tales   75

Reflecting on the strike years later, Carl Chamberlain wrote the following, previously unpublished, poem:

Strike

Brother against Brother
Throwing bricks of hate
Strangers shouting, fighting at the pit gate
While mothers shuffle to the corner shop
Living off the slate
Then the Marches, Rallies
Proud union banners waving through the rain
Battles were fought like a civil war
Now we all pretend we can't remember
How much it meant to us
Just what it all stood for.

Geoff Blore:
"I still have mates from my mining days. Some went on strike but others didn't. We don't talk about it, not because we'd fall out but I think the ones who didn't strike are embarrassed now. In the end we all got the chop."

The Closures
'A job for life'
Between 1984 and 1989, mining jobs declined nationally from 181,000 to 66,000. So the aftermath of the strike brought with it not only broken

Demolition of Hucknall no. 2 headstocks in June 1989. 'A thunderous explosion was heard all over town.' (Hucknall Dispatch)

76   Nottinghamshire Miners' Tales

friendships but great stress and uncertainty.
Carl:
"...A job for life.... The first thing we knew about that (closure) was when one or two of the big Coal Board men came and we knew something was happening then. Then we'd get all brought together, announcements in the canteen, there's going to be a major meeting at so and so. And then you would start seeing news crews again in town, BBC vans and ITV, Central news. You'd think there's something big going on here."

The first poem Carl wrote describes vividly what happened next.

Hucknall No.2

A meeting to be held, all men to attend
Rumours fly like bullets, wounding some yet others go unscathed
Amidst trestle tables and folding chairs
The inevitable is announced
Transfers are discussed and papers signed
Lifetimes spent working together are dissolved by shaking rough black
*   nailed hands*
So sweep the empty snuff tins
Hose the black dust filled spit
Leave it just the way we found it
The Suit and Tie has just repeated
'There's no future at this pit.'

After the closure was announced, some things that happened next seemed to be absolute madness.
Carl:
"…. At Hucknall they had what they called a prep. plant, where they would wash and grade the coal. They were actually building one end while the demolition crews were starting to knock down the other. It was a 7 million quid investment, a contract that had been signed for. It was a farcical waste of money."
When Linby closed shortly after, there were 3,000 men out of work in the area.

Carl:

Job Centre

We sit in rows clutching white cards
Though it's no one's birthday
Applying for positions we've no experience in
Packers and Porters
Stackers and Sorters
Wages and hours negotiable
We play the party games
Blind man's bluff
Postman's knock on Wednesdays
Brings more Monopoly money
Throw a six to start again.

Carl took a transfer to Bestwood Workshops:

Carl Chamberlain

"I'd just bought this house. Just come from a small terraced house…. But I didn't like it at the Workshops. It was like being in a factory…. Repetitive and the atmosphere weren't the same. (Later he worked for a builder but there was little demand in what was now a depressed area). I work ironically about 50 yards from where I used to work before at Inkermans Auto Electrical. It backs on to the pit site. There are some surveyors on it now so I don't know whether somebody's going to do something. There were rumours of a supermarket, petrol station and a McDonald's which provides about 20 jobs doesn't it? I don't think there's that many jobs for youngsters.
I think a lot of the trouble with young kids today is the fact that nobody knows them… before somebody would say, 'Your lad were mucking about on the market last Friday. Have a word with him tomorrow.' And he'd say, 'Oh, was he? Right.'"

The reason given for closing Hucknall was a large fault in the limestone which would be too difficult and expensive to overcome but Carl says:
"We don't know do we?"

Six months after Hucknall closed, it was the turn of Newstead. Geoff Blore had already taken redundancy but he remembers his astonishment at the news:
"They said the deputies had voted to close the pit but we had always been told that there was twenty years more coal there."

Linby closed in the autumn of 1987 followed by Mansfield in the spring of 1988. Mansfield had become the largest town in England without a railway station when the Great Central station closed in January, 1956 and the Midland station in 1964. But with a crisis looming the town desperately needed a good public transport system.

The scale of job losses was enormous and took place when there was a recession and the county had a higher unemployment rate than average. In 1989 over 33% of all male employees in the Mansfield area worked in the coal industry and it was estimated that the loss of the pit plus the knock-on effects could push male unemployment in the area up to 40%.

Eastwood – the End of an Era
'…. If you come from Moorgreen we'll set you on.'
Already, local and county councils had had to deal with a serious situation in Eastwood for, after centuries of mining going back into the middle ages, the town was facing the end of an era. In a tribute entitled *'Moorgreen Colliery 1865 to 1985'* the NCB explains:
'…. Early this century there were 19 working (pits) within three miles of the centre of the town – a town with many historical associations with the growth of the industrial revolution in the 19th century, the birth of the Midland Railway and the ever present memory of D. H. Lawrence. He once described the area as '…. The coal blasted countryside,' and the pits as 'like black studs linked together by the loop of fine chain, the railway.'

The booklet also goes on to comment :
'…. The people who worked there were recognised as among the best. It used to be said: '…. If you come from Moorgreen, we'll set you on.'
But this was written just before the pit closures in the rest of the county, so there is a sad irony in the talk of:
'…. The potential for further growth in the coalfield and the leading part the county will play in supplying Britain's energy needs into the next century.'

The closing of a pit because there was no more coal was a state of affairs which miners understood and were familiar with, but they could no longer migrate to other coalfields. In this case there had, however, been plenty of warning and the imaginative Eastwood Phoenix Project had been set up. Today the site of Moorgreen is called Colliers Wood, and the countryside is being restored. The town has capitalised on the reputation of its most famous son, D.H. Lawrence, with a permanent exhibition at Durban House and a tourist trail which includes the house in which Lawrence was born. Local county councillor Sir Dennis Pettit explained also that courses were run for the unemployed and youngsters to train them for "*for proper jobs not just "MacDonalds" jobs.*" There was hardship at Eastwood but not the bitterness facing the rest of the County.

Trouble in the Council Chamber
The controlling Labour Group at County Hall faced serious problems as a result of the strike and the mounting number of closures. However, the differences caused by the union split had to be dealt with.
Councillor Sir Dennis Pettit was quoted in Peter Housden's book *'Local Statesmen.'*:
"The worst time for me in terms of unity of the Group was the 84-85 strike. We had striking miners, we had UDM miners in the same Group. In one Group meeting one of our members threw one of these heavy ashtrays across the chamber to hit somebody on the other side. Fortunately he missed. If you look at the old Labour Group in those days, a large chunk of it belonged to the mining community... We had people like Alf Burton, the Chief Whip, who was NUM through and through, but he was level-headed about the UDM. He knew the main point was the unity of the Group."

The Groggs

The figures of miners which appear at the start of each chapter in the book are produced by Richard Hughes of Pontypridd.

'The Collier' was based on Richard Hughes, namesake and great-grandfather of the Groggs' creator. He was a repairer in the Albion Colliery in Cilfynydd and was killed in an accident underground in 1901.

'Crouching Miner' was based on George Crocker.

'Breakfast Underground' was based on Charlie Crocker, who bred canaries.

'Collier Boy' was based on Richard Hughes himself as a boy.

'Father & Son' was based on George Davies, the man who remarried Richard's great-grandmother Hughes, and was himself blinded in the colliery.

'Miner & Pit Pony' was based on Richard Hughes.

PART NINE: The final decade

The Robin Hood Line
'One of the most successful commuter lines in the region.'

Group unity was to be increasingly important as the council tackled the grave situation caused by the pit closures. One bold move was the proposed re-opening of the Robin Hood Line. The line had run 32 miles in all, but there were big complications to be overcome, for parts of it had been severed and tunnels had been filled in and, in the course of complex agreements and negotiations, the railways were privatised. It took determination and commitment on the part of those guiding the local and county councils through the maze of requirements to see the project through. Stage one was opened in May 1993. Stage two, which was the link to Mansfield, was opened in 1995, and the completed line to Worksop in 1998. The line serves 300,000 people, is one of the most successful commuter lines in the region, and still receives a subsidy from Notts County Council. But before all of this was complete, there was a further blow to the mining industry.

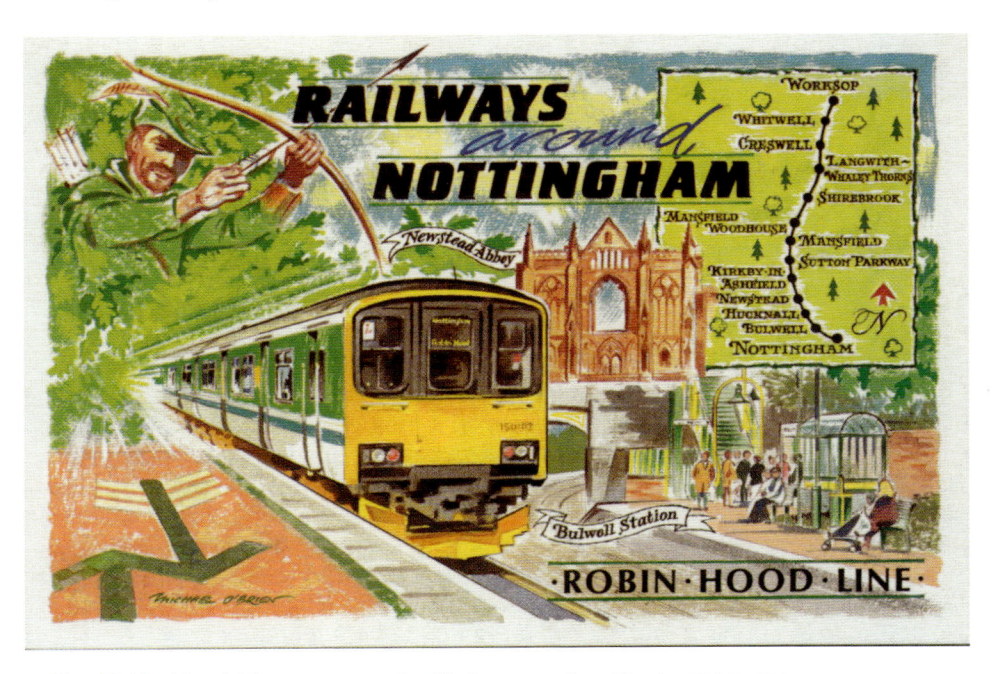

The Robin Hood Line, re-opened with its evocative title in 1995. This postcard was designed by Radcliffe-on-Trent artist Michael O'Brien. The original design was amended when the line was extended to Worksop in 1998

Nottinghamshire Miners' Tales

The Challenge
'And we knew it was only a matter of time before Cotgrave would go.'
Stan recalls the uncertainty of the years after the first closures:
"The problem was that when it was announced, it was announced on such a big scale. I don't think people could believe what was happening. And I mean it was like one pit after another and before you knew it there was no pits. And it was only a matter of time before we knew Cotgrave would go and we sat on the fence like that for two years thinking we'll be gone in six months. Nobody would spend any money. Everybody was in the same position. 'I want to move house but I daren't.' 'I want a new car but I daren't.' 'I want to buy this for the house but I daren't' And in the end this went on for years, putting the families under stress, the wives under stress. And people that had moved and took bigger mortgages, they were the ones that fell down in the end because they'd already moved and then they tell you the pit's going to close and they're mortgaged up to the hilt – never recovered from it really.'

On October 13th 1992 British Coal announced that a further 31 pits nationally would close. An announcement that was greeted by *'incredulity and anger not only in Nottinghamshire but nationally.'* The surviving mines in Nottinghamshire were Annesley/Bentinck, Harworth, Manton, Ollerton, Thoresby and Welbeck. Under review were Bevercotes, Bilsthorpe, Calverton, Clipstone and Rufford and the two threatened with immediate closure were Cotgrave and Silverhill. Cotgrave was described as having *'an appalling cost history .'* NACODS disputed this and said that, despite current difficulties, Cotgrave had good future prospects.

In *'The case for British coal. THE CASE FOR COTGRAVE.'* a report compiled on behalf of Cotgrave Town Council and the *Cotgrave Matters* Campaign, arguments were put forward in defence of all the threatened pits. The slogan was:
'SAVE THE PIT. Save the community.'

The Coalfield Enquiry
The County Council, with the support of all political groups, set up a public hearing under the independent chairmanship of (Sir) Anthony Scrivener QC. It was called 'The Nottinghamshire Coalfield Enquiry' and acted as a forum for all interested parties across the county. It took place at County Hall on the 12th to the 14th of November 1992. The published document consists of two volumes, each over one inch thick, and apart from a summary and other details there were 76 appendices presented at the meeting. In his opening remarks, Leader of the council, councillor (Sir) Dennis Pettit stated

'..... Many heartfelt protests have been made and strong feelings have been expressed in a truly impressive variety of ways. The challenge we now face is to convince the powers that be that there has to be a future for coal.

.....Those who do not give our coal industry a real chance to compete and survive must realise that, in places like Nottinghamshire, they will not be easily forgiven.'

(Sir) Anthony Scrivener:
'I hope I have managed to capture the intensity of feeling and anger universally expressed by all the witnesses against these proposals in this short report.'
The witnesses were of all shades of political opinion and from all walks of life including mining experts, bishops, academics and social workers.

By 1992, twelve pits in Nottinghamshire had been closed and 40,000 jobs had been lost, 27,000 in mining alone, but the area had received no special government help. The average age of the mining workforce was 34 years, so early retirement was not an option. Now, once more, thousands of jobs were threatened. Soon the £5 million weekly wages from the British Coal would be lost to the local economy plus an estimated £9 million in rates paid annually to local councils.

Some Important Conclusions
'The dash for gas'
One important conclusion the Enquiry reached was that after Electricity was privatised:
'a fundamental shift in electricity generation from coal to gas, which is the single most important factor in the threat to coal, has come about without public debate and without public policy.'
This became known as 'the dash for gas.' To add to this, coal was being imported from the USA, Poland and Colombia. And it was the Colombian coal which raised the most questions because of that country's poor record on child labour in mining.
At the Enquiry the NUM voiced the question which continues to trouble many people:
'Why did the government wish to throw away the industry after such huge investment and many sacrifices by the miners?'
In her report to the Enquiry, Rita Sharpe, Coalfield Development Officer, Notts Rural Community Council, summarises the reactions of a stunned and demoralised mining community:
"We used to have a sense of belonging."
"We used to care about each other."
"Nobody cares about us."
"The heart's gone."
"It's the young ones I feel most sorry for. What have they got to look forward to?"
She concludes: *'Coal is not just a commodity, it is a culture.'*
But the closures went ahead.
Stan:
"I can always remember thinking I can't believe I'm going into the pit for my last time and it was so weird driving up the yard for the last time."

Bilsthorpe

On 18th August, 1993, there came a tragic reminder of the true cost of coal when an extensive roof fall occurred at Bilsthorpe Colliery. The HSE Report states:

'The fall occurred at the 1032m. measuring mark and extended inbye (direction away from the main shaft or surface outlet) over a length of 46m. It involved the whole width of the roadway and at its extremities contained a great deal of broken rock debris.'

Inbye end of a fall at Bilsthorpe in 1993 (Stationery Office)

The fall was at 10.58 a.m. By 13.39, members of the Mansfield Mines Rescue were assisting at the scene. Six men were trapped. Three of them escaped but three died. Recovering the bodies was extremely difficult and Mansfield Mines Rescue received a special plaque from the family of one of the deceased, Peter W. Alcock, thanking them for their bravery.

By January 1st 1995 the mines were returned to private ownership. Nationalisation had lasted 48 years. When the Annesley/Bentinck complex closed in January 2000 there were only four working pits left in the county; Clipstone, Welbeck, Thoresby and Harworth, employing between them less than 2,000 men, and to date Clipstone's future is uncertain.

Moving On
'You are all together and that's like being in the army.'

Mining was a tough and dangerous job, but there are still things about it which are missed.

Stan:
"Definitely the people. They were a different type of people down the mines and I think if you met any miner they'll tell you the same. I mean I'm working with a lot of miners now, which is great, and they all miss it in different ways. I miss it for the people and I miss it for the satisfaction of the job. But the people's humour down there! Amazing people. You'd always get the grumpy ones but 90% of miners were very witty because with the job you were doing you had to be. Everybody hated the job but it was alright on pay day especially if you'd been asked to do Big Three, that was Saturday morning,

Sunday morning, go back Sunday night but when you got your pay packet it was 'oh I'm alright I've got Big Three in my pay packet'."
Geoff:
"The comradeship, that's what I miss."
Norman:
"The crack (banter). The brilliant one-liners. But you know no-one should have to do that job."
Let Carl sum it up:
"I think it was working in the face of adversity. I fell off that little wall out there when I was gardening once and I done me ligaments in me ankle and the ambulance man come out. I couldn't move. Real bad. And he says, 'What do you do mate?' and I says I'm a miner and he says, 'Oh it's like being in the army isn't it? You know what I mean. You are all together and that's like being in the army.' And I said yes, it is in a way."

In Nottinghamshire you're only a handshake away from a miner. Like the Scarlet Pimpernel they are everywhere - look closely at local policemen, councillors, craftsmen and tradesmen, nurses and salesmen and you'll soon find them. There are poets, playwrights and booksellers, too, not to mention a gamekeeper!

Geoff Blore opened a bookshop on Mansfield Road after leaving Newstead. Always an avid reader, his first stock consisted mainly of his collection of travel books. The shop is still there, but nowadays Geoff is to be found at Jermy and Westerman on Mansfield Road.

Norman and Jean still live near the Mines Rescue Station at Ashby de la Zouch from which Norman retired. When interviewed, he enjoyed talking about the old days, but was also enthusiastic about his new job as a gamekeeper.

Sid Radford passed away in February 2001. He and Madge were married for over sixty years. She misses him and grieves for him.

George Burton lives at Whitwick. He is keenly interested in local history and also the history of the Mines Rescue Service.

Neal Kirk, though almost 75, can still *'walk a ball around a golf course.'*

Barry Heath has enjoyed great success as a playwright and to date three of his plays have been produced at the Nottingham Playhouse. The programme for his 1999 work, *'Rats, Buckets and Bombs.'* contains the following comments;
'With his new play 'Rats, Buckets and Bombs' we are thrilled to welcome back Mansfield writer Barry Heath who was last at the Playhouse in the

1980's. His smash-hit productions of 'Me Mam Sez' and 'Y'Shunta Joined! ' both had audiences queuing round the block for tickets....'

Stan Stanton works in the motor industry and still takes part in sport but it's golf these days rather than rugby.

Carl Chamberlain continues to write poetry:
" knew a big change was about to start in the pit communities when the mines began to shut, and I suppose in my naive way I tried to document what was happening at that time. There was not a lot you could do, but trying to write it all down was at least something."
His first poem 'Hucknall No 2' won the Nottingham Festival Competition. To date he has written on a variety of topics, has been published in newspapers and magazines and had short stories featured on BBC Radio Nottingham and Radio Mansfield.

Reclamation and Memorials
In its 1999 report the County Council explains:
'The coal industry, with its vast spoil tips, literally spoiled some of the areas of the west and centre of the county. The pitheads are now all but gone and eight of the remaining coal tips are being reclaimed and landscaped by the County Council following a £10 million deal with British Coal and the Forestry Commission. The project includes the biggest tree planting in lowland Britain for 30 years. The former Warsop Colliery, Boughton Camp and Linby Colliery have all been reclaimed and transformed by the County Council.'

In some places the fight continues as those interested in conservation engage in 'The battle to save the wildlife of Bentinck Void' so that the site of the former opencast mine does not become a landfill area.
However, the County Council still plays a 'leading part in the Coalfield Communities Campaign, an organisation linking coalmining areas across Britain and lobbying hard at home and in Europe for a fair deal and a brighter future for Britain's coalmining areas.' It still has to grapple with the problems caused by the loss of coalmining and the collapse of other traditional industries such as textiles reflected in 'closed shops and pubs and boarded up houses.... And poorer performance than expected at school by young people.' For while some former mining areas such as Eastwood have made a good recovery, other old colliery villages continue to struggle. But encouraging news was announced in the Nottingham Evening Post, August 16th, 2001:
'£300,000 for former mining towns.
Blowing dust off the coalfields. More than 400 new jobs could be created in former mining areas of Notts thanks to a £300,000 cash injection. The North Notts and North Derbyshire Coalfield Alliance has secured the cash from the Government's Single Regeneration Budget. And it is hoping to use the

money to encourage new firms to set up business in the area. It has launched a three year action plan and set itself a target of creating 400 new jobs in areas such as Mansfield, Sutton-in-Ashfield and Ollerton.'
Another project is the Nottingham Express Transit (NET) which, in the case, for instance, of Hucknall, holds out great hope for the future.
Neil Bates, Executive Director NET Project writes in a newsletter:
'Hucknall, like many towns which were built and grew on the coal industry has fought valiantly to maintain the vibrancy of the local economy. Nottingham Express Transit is just the development Hucknall needs to build on these efforts, by providing a new link to and from Hucknall which will help to attract more and more investment into the area.'

Ex-miners have expressed their disappointment at the lack of suitable memorials and the haste with which all evidence of mining has vanished. Demolition teams often moved in before the last shift finished. It seemed as if everyone wanted to forget that:
'Britain (even the Royal Navy) had for a century depended on a prospering and courageous coal industry.'
In Hucknall, ex-miner John Wheeldon is reported in the Hucknall Despatch of 27th September, 1996 as being:
"outraged at an 'insulting' small black wheel put up by British Coal in a remote part of Wigwam Lane."
Similar comments can still be heard as ex-miners react to the "Meccano" being erected as memorials instead of the original powerful winding wheels which once dominated the countryside.
Perhaps the most delightful tribute though is the stained glass panel, one of four, unveiled earlier this year (2001) at the entrance to County Hall in West Bridgford, which features the headstocks and is a graceful reminder of Nottinghamshire's past. The panels have been completed by a circle of Eastwood ladies known as the ESCAPE Group (Eastwood Senior Citizens Art Project Enterprise) under the guidance of stained glass artist Deb Mawby. More references to coal mining can be seen in another of their windows, which has recently been installed in the council chamber at Eastwood. Many of the ladies are miners' widows and have their own stories to tell about life in a mining community.

The Future of Coalmining in Nottinghamshire
'…. Not in my lifetime but probably in my grandchildren's lifetime.'
The Mines Rescue Service Ltd. (MRSL)
Paul Wilkinson:
"We still look after the teams from the mines but it doesn't take up as much of our time. We do more work with big companies. I had to go up to Glasgow airport last August to help with a training session. When I walked into the big hangar full of all these planes I felt like a little boy. It was quite an experience."

Extract from MRSL leaflet:
'Rescue of persons from aircraft fuel tanks (MRSL). On 1st August 2000, at Glasgow airport and under the scrutiny of British Airways, Mines Rescue personnel successfully recovered a simulated asphyxiated casualty from the actual wing tank of a Boeing 737-200, having first applied resuscitation equipment within 3 minutes, followed by full extrication within 7 minutes, all the emphasis being given to patient care and stabilisation.'

Mick Noble:
"The procedure was developed here at Mansfield. Last November I went to Seattle to supervise the training of personnel there and British Airways told me that other companies would follow suit. So far we've had enquiries from two big airlines. I wouldn't mind doing the training for Quantas.
Thus, a number of big companies recognise the hundred years of experience Mines Rescue Services have had of extricating those trapped in confined places. Besides British Airways, MRSL have devised procedures for Rolls Royce, British Sugar and other 'blue chip' companies.

Meanwhile, mining in Nottinghamshire, though still a dangerous job, has become highly sophisticated. The old colliers would hardly recognise a modern coal face or the machinery used under ground.
UK Coal has plans for development but what do the ex-miners predict for the coal industry in the county?
Ex-miners:
"There will be no mines in Nottinghamshire in five years time."
Carl :
"It's finished."
But Stan has a different idea:
"They'll come back. They have to. Not in my lifetime but in my grandchildren's lifetime they'll be mining throughout Nottinghamshire once again when the oil and gas have gone. There's billions of tons of coal under there and they're going to need it."

But whatever the future holds, one thing is certain, Nottinghamshire gained more from the pits than just coal.

Memorial for the mining industry: stained glass window at County Hall, West Bridgford

Welbeck Abbey, owned by the Duke of Portland, on a picture postcard view from 1910

Thoresby Hall. Lord Manvers was not pleased with the arrival of coal mining in the 1920s.

Nottinghamshire Miners' Tales

Miners leaving one of the last shifts at Moorgreen Colliery in 1985 (National Coal Board)

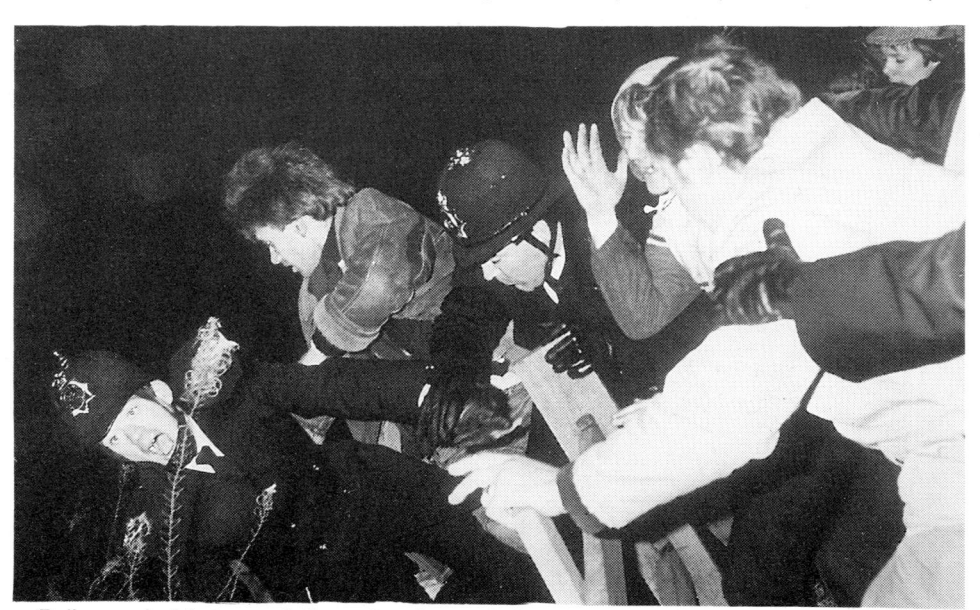

Police and pickets crash through a fence during their struggle at Thoresby Colliery in March 1984 (National Museum of Labour History)

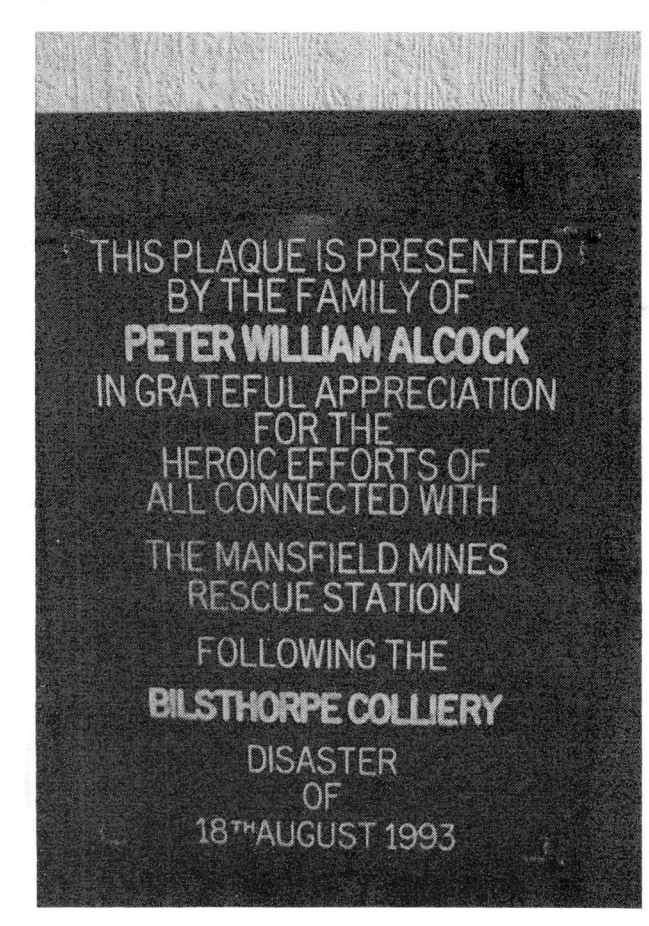

No explanation needed: a thankyou plaque at Mansfield

THIS PLAQUE IS PRESENTED
BY THE FAMILY OF
PETER WILLIAM ALCOCK
IN GRATEFUL APPRECIATION
FOR THE
HEROIC EFFORTS OF
ALL CONNECTED WITH

THE MANSFIELD MINES
RESCUE STATION

FOLLOWING THE

BILSTHORPE COLLIERY
DISASTER
OF
18TH AUGUST 1993

Below: commemorative Cotgrave Colliery plates (Stan Stanton collection).
There are stained glass windows in Cotgrave Church, showing the colliery headstocks and coal seams as a memorial to the local pit

Nottinghamshire Miners' Tales

It's all over: the site of Cotgrave Colliery. Parts of this are being converted to a country park, but people are still being warned to keep off this area

Cover illustrations: (1) an exercise in the underground gallery at the original Rescue Station in Mansfield Woodhouse (2) a Martyn Pitt photo for UK Coal

Welbeck Abbey, owned by the Duke of Portland, on a picture postcard view from 1910

Thoresby Hall. Lord Manvers was not pleased with the arrival of coal mining in the 1920s.

Nottinghamshire Miners' Tales

Miners leaving one of the last shifts at Moorgreen Colliery in 1985 (National Coal Board)

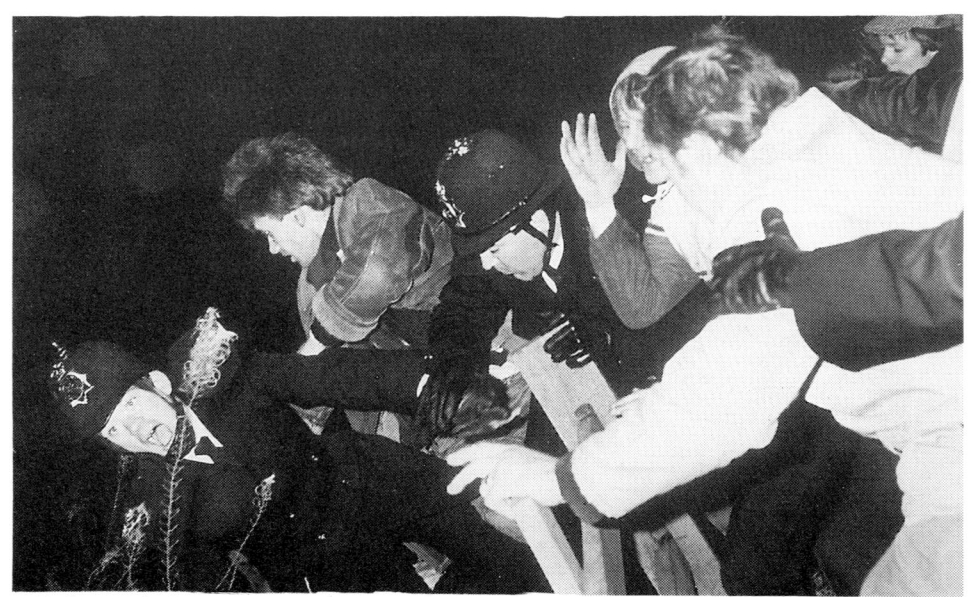

Police and pickets crash through a fence during their struggle at Thoresby Colliery in March 1984 (National Museum of Labour History)

THIS PLAQUE IS PRESENTED
BY THE FAMILY OF
PETER WILLIAM ALCOCK
IN GRATEFUL APPRECIATION
FOR THE
HEROIC EFFORTS OF
ALL CONNECTED WITH

THE MANSFIELD MINES
RESCUE STATION

FOLLOWING THE

BILSTHORPE COLLIERY

DISASTER
OF
18TH AUGUST 1993

No explanation needed: a thankyou plaque at Mansfield

Below: commemorative Cotgrave Colliery plates (Stan Stanton collection).
There are stained glass windows in Cotgrave Church, showing the colliery headstocks and coal seams as a memorial to the local pit

It's all over: the site of Cotgrave Colliery. Parts of this are being converted to a country park, but people are still being warned to keep off this area

Cover illustrations: (1) an exercise in the underground gallery at the original Rescue Station in Mansfield Woodhouse (2) a Martyn Pitt photo for UK Coal

92   Nottinghamshire Miners' Tales